365 DAYS of

UNICORNS

HOW TO DRAW UNICORNS AND FRIENDS EVERY DAY OF THE YEAR

EASY STEP-BY-STEP DRAWING

CLÉMENTINE DERODIT

DAVID & CHARLES

www.davidandcharles.com

Welcome to the wonderful world of unicorns and their friends!

In this book, you will find a huge range of drawings!
To help you navigate, you'll find a symbol at the top of each page to indicate the theme.

 Discover an endless array of different unicorns!

Explore kawaii objects, buildings, food and scenery from the unicorns' magical land!

 Meet all of the unicorns' cute and funny friends!

Communicate with the unicorns through funny letters and pretty designs – they even have their own emoticons!

The secrets of kawaii drawing

Use a pencil to create your drawings. Some lines will need to be erased.

 1 Use simple shapes (shown in blue) to start your drawing.

 2 Continue by adding details bit by bit. These appear in red at each step so that you can easily spot them.

 3 Use the blue marks to guide you when drawing the facial details.

 4 Go over the outlines with markers. Use lots of colours – it's more fun! Erase the construction lines when the ink is dry to prevent it bleeding.

 5 Colour with markers or coloured pencils and add small patterns around your drawing. Wow!

Which colours to choose?

Unicorns ride rainbows!
Bright or pastel – which range do you prefer?

You can also use metallic or glitter gel pens to make your unicorns and all your other cute drawings shine!

Cute Unicorn

Let the great unicorn parade begin!

Winged Unicorn

Sitting Unicorn

Rearing Unicorn

Flamboyant Unicorn

Celestial Unicorn

Romantic Unicorn

Floating Unicorn

Loving Unicorn

Cupid Unicorn

Meditating Unicorn

Thoughtful Unicorn

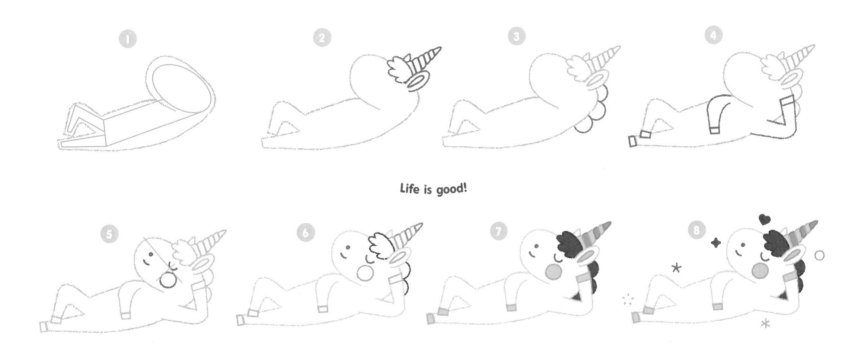

Life is good!

Tired Unicorn

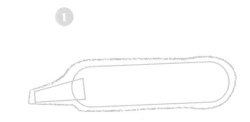

Sleeping Unicorn

Dreaming Unicorn

Angel Unicorn

Babushka Unicorn

Dala Unicorn

Piñata Unicorn

Fairground Unicorn

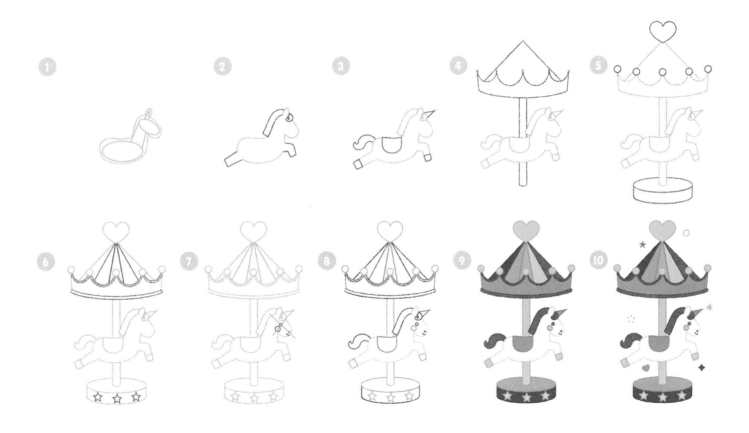

Skipping Unicorn

Hula-Hooping Unicorn

Horse-Riding Unicorn

What a funny sight!

Rocking Unicorn

Wobble Unicorn

Roller-Skating Unicorn

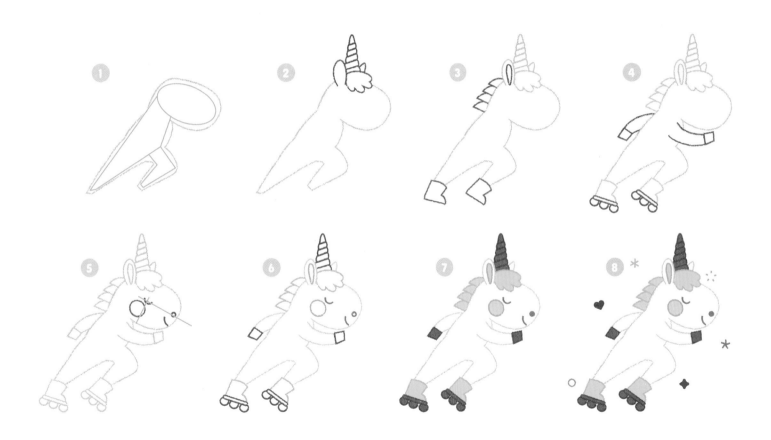

Ice-Skating Unicorn

Ice-Dancing Unicorn

Skateboarding Unicorn

Scooting Unicorn

Boxing Unicorn

Footballing Unicorn

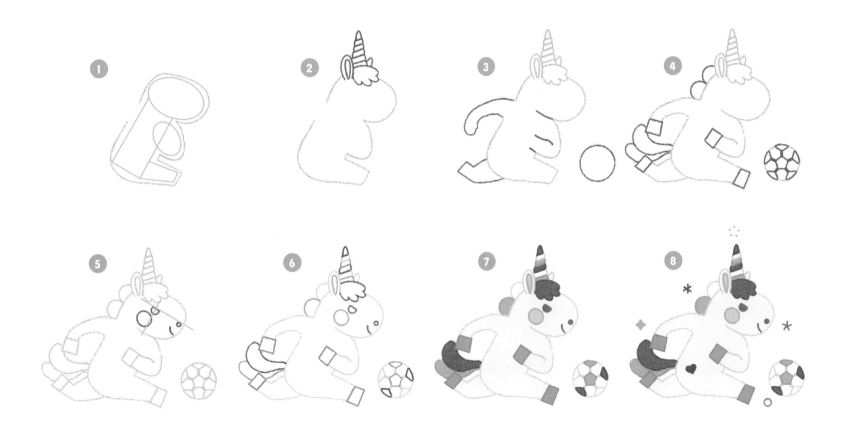

Unicorn in a Plane

Unicorn in a Car

Ballerina Unicorn

Dancing Unicorn

Unicorns love to dance and play!

Breakdancing Unicorn

Hula Girl Unicorn

Dabbing Unicorn

Cheerleading Unicorn

Rockstar Unicorn

Guitarist Unicorn

Bling Unicorn

Punk Unicorn

Artist Unicorn

Cartoon Unicorn

Unicorn of Love

Unicorn on a Cloud

Unicorn in a Hat

Unicorn in a Helmet

Unicorn with a Bouquet

Flower-Horned Unicorn

Candle-Horned Unicorn

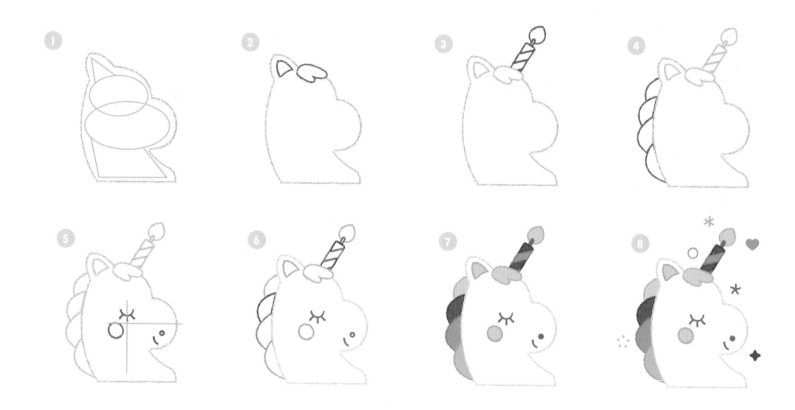

Rainbow-Horned Unicorn

Happy Unicorn

Intrigued Unicorn

Sad Unicorn

Angry Unicorn

Are you sometimes in a bad mood?

Clown Unicorn

Cowboy Unicorn

Frida Unicorn

Queen's Guard Unicorn

Unicorn in a Beret

Unicorn on Holiday

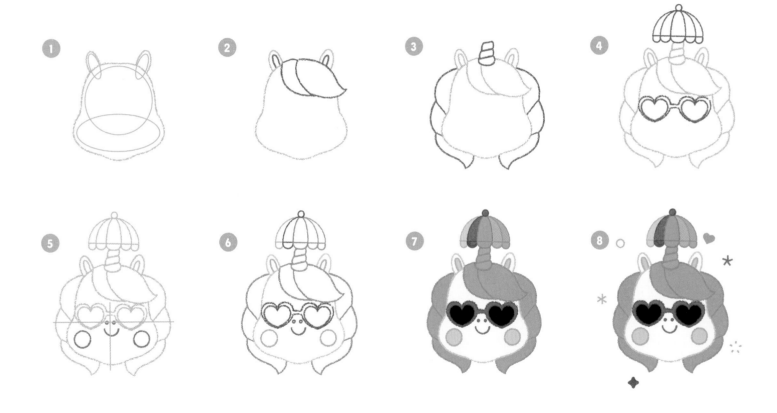

Diving Unicorn

Snorkelling Unicorn

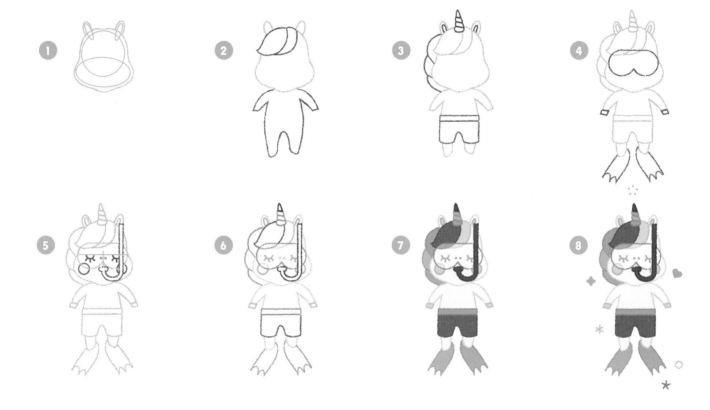

Rainy Day Unicorn

Unicorn in the Bath

Halloween Unicorn

Ghostie Unicorn

Not even scary!

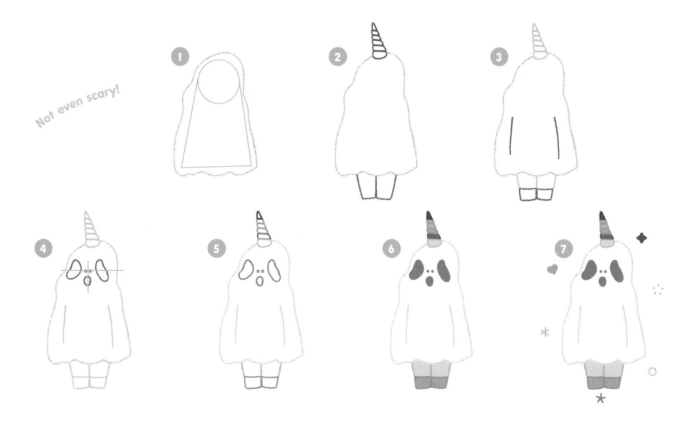

Cinco de Mayo Unicorn

Pumpkin Unicorn

Snowman Unicorn

Santa Unicorn

Hobby-Horse Unicorn

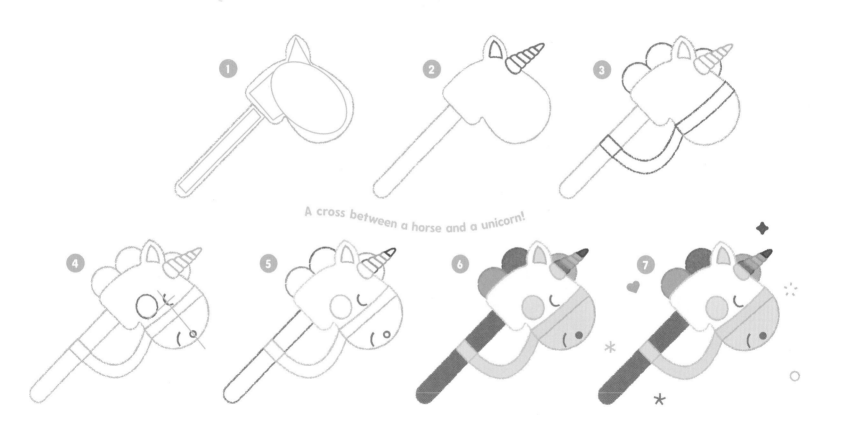

A cross between a horse and a unicorn!

Christmas Unicorn

Baker Unicorn

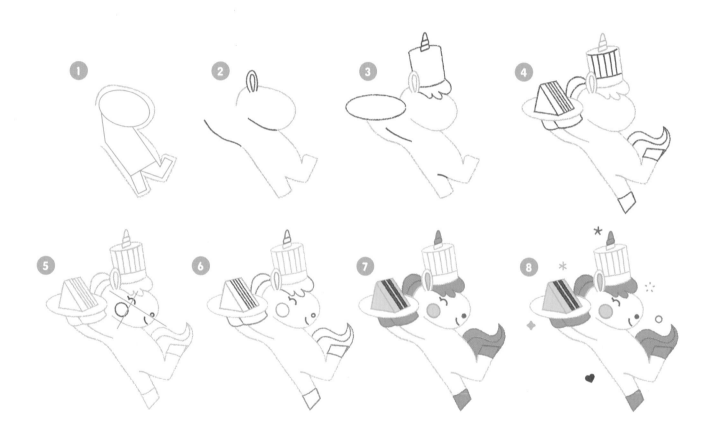

Unicorn Cake

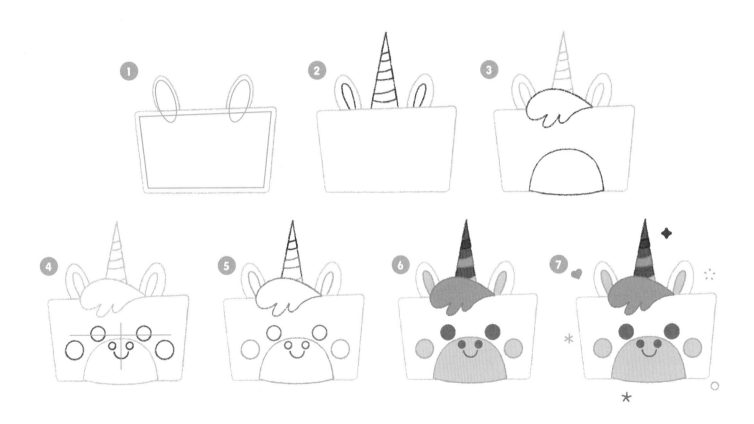

Chess-Piece Unicorn

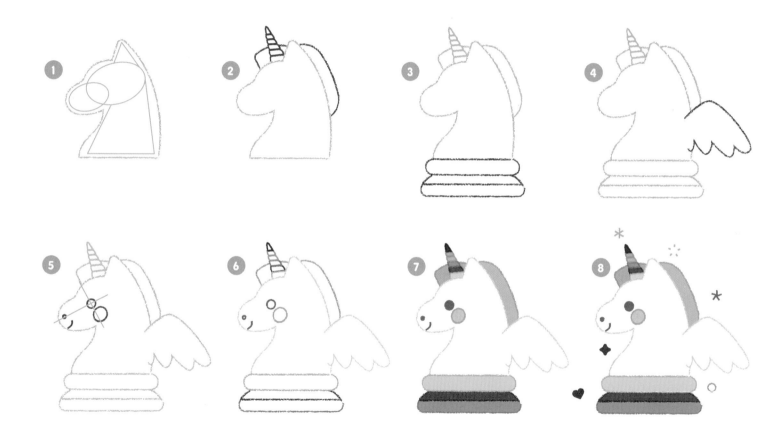

Dinosaur Unicorn

Mermaid Unicorn

Dragon Unicorn

Astronaut Unicorn

Unicorn UFO

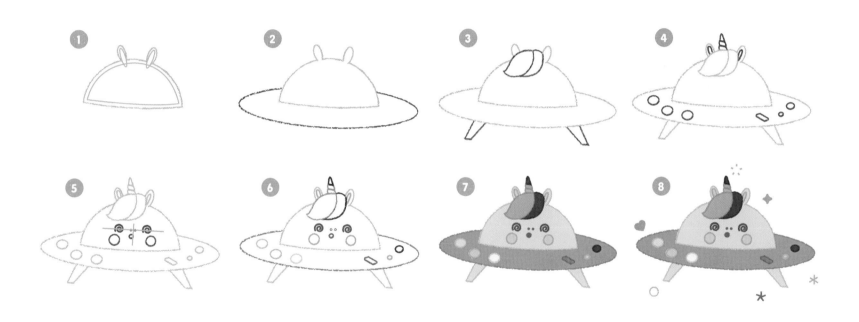

Pixel Unicorn

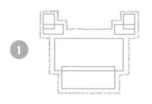

1

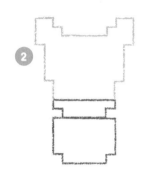

2

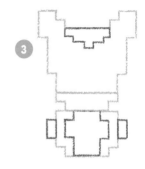

3

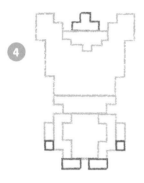

4

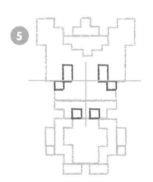

5

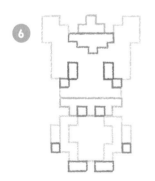

6

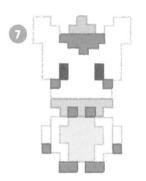

7

8

Gaming Unicorn

Unicorn Selfie

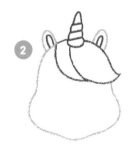

I love taking pictures of myself!

Reading Unicorn

Party Unicorn

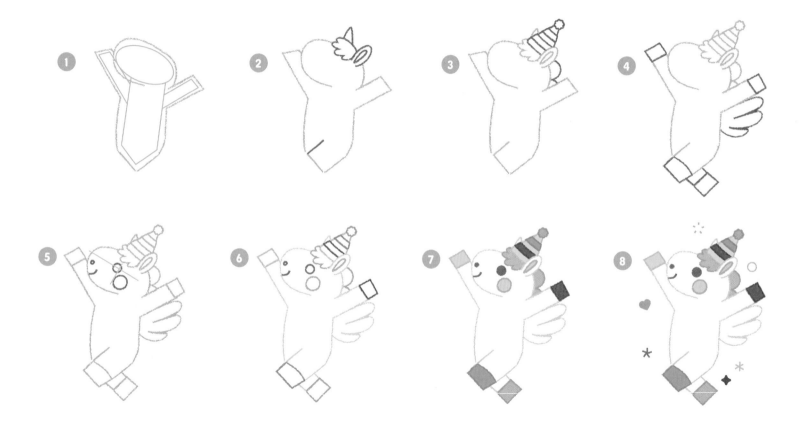

Kimono Unicorn

Baby Unicorn

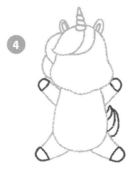

Unicorn Twins

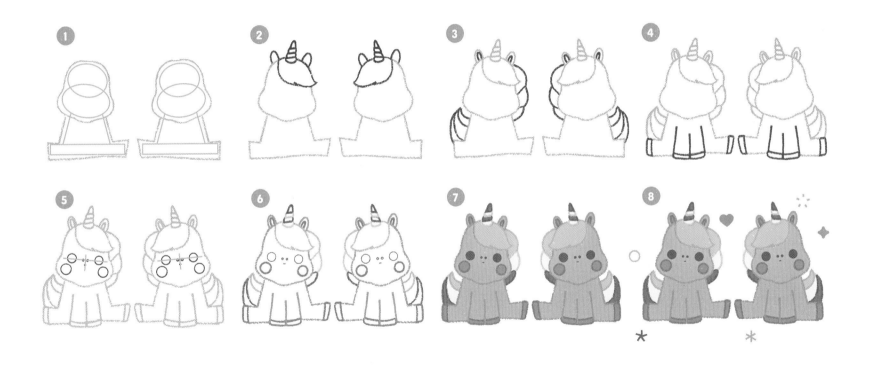

Windy Unicorn

Unicorn Poop

Yes, even unicorns have to poop!

Candy House

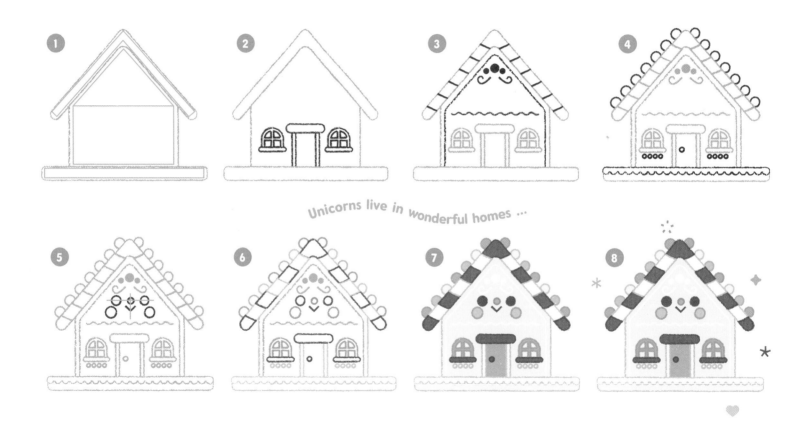

Unicorns live in wonderful homes ...

Gingerbread House

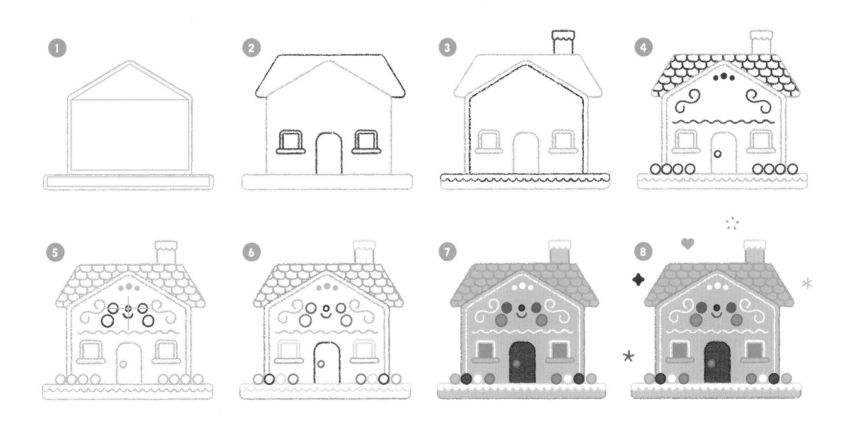

Windmill

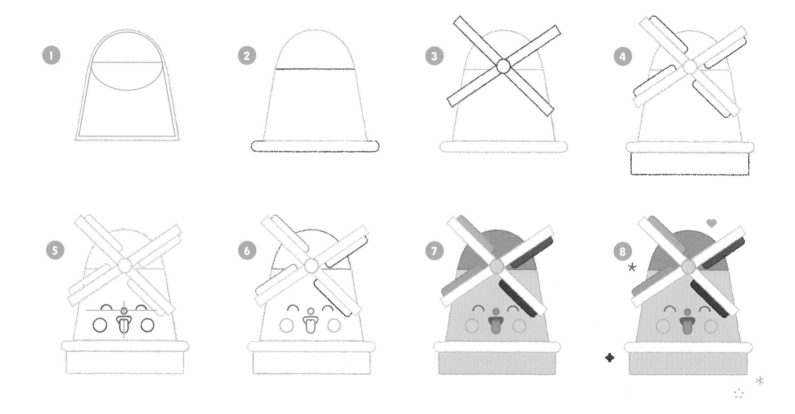

Apple Tree

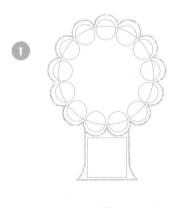

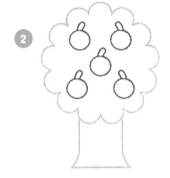

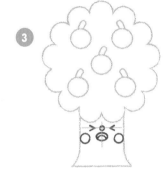

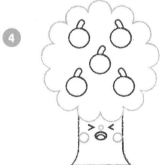

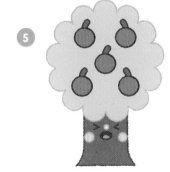

Enchanted Forest

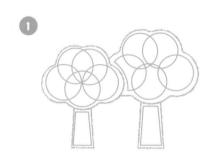

1

2

3

4

5

6

Magic Car

Cat-ctus

Sad Cactus

Spring Flower

Tulip

Sunflower

Rose

What a lovely smell!

Lotus Flower

Flower Pot

Acorn

Apple

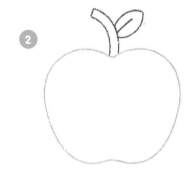

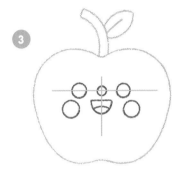

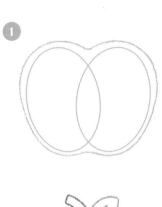

Strawberry

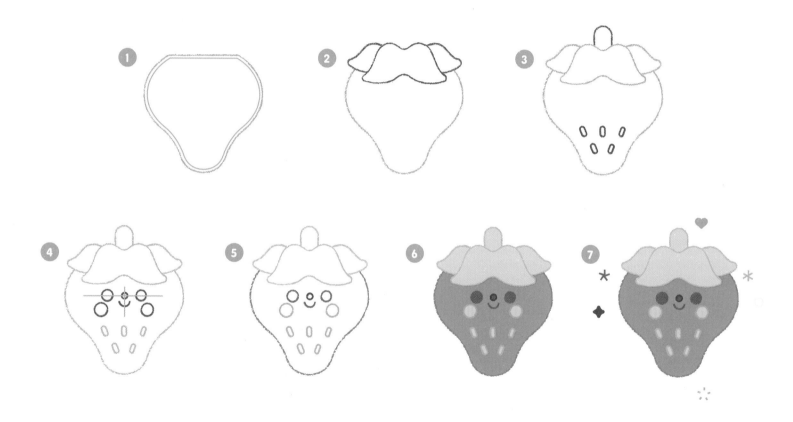

Orange

Banana

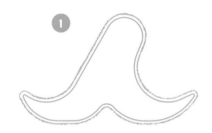

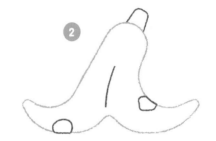

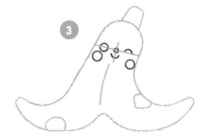

Carrot

Broken Egg

1

2

3

4

5

6

Egg Timer

Frying Pan

Noodles

Sushi

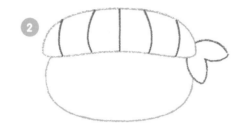

Mmm ... looks delicious!

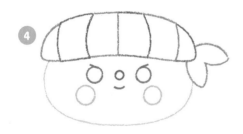

Onigiri

Hot Dog

Hamburger

Pizza

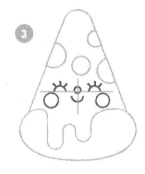

Popcorn

Cupcake

Donut

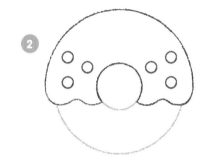

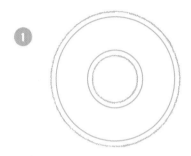

Cookie

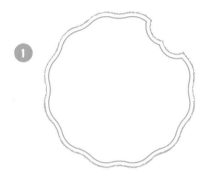

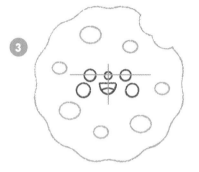

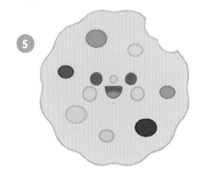

Gingerbread Man

Muffin

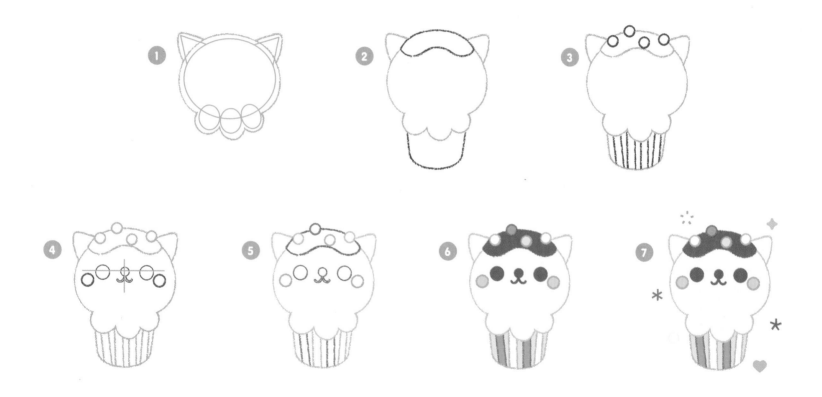

Croissant

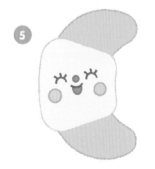

133

Pudding

Chocolate Cake

Unicorns can't get enough!

Rainbow Cake

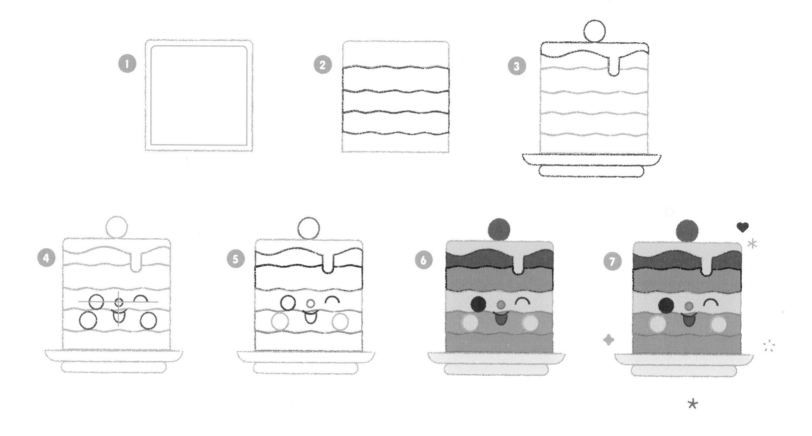

Slice of Cake

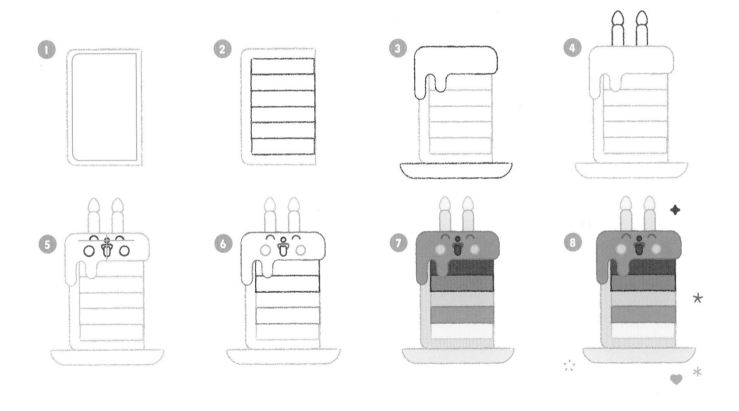

Whippy Ice Cream

Ice Cream Cone

Ice Cream Sundae

Bowl of Ice Cream

Cotton Candy

Sweet

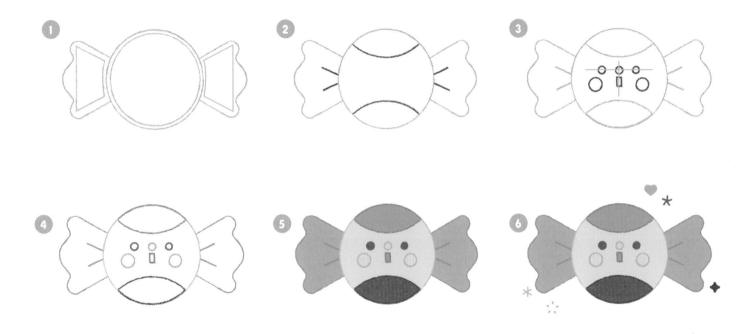

Lollipop

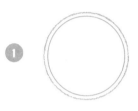

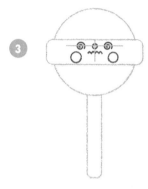

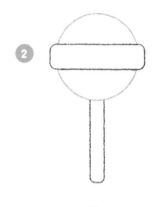

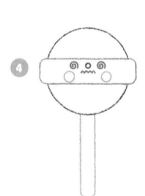

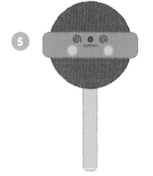

144

Milkshake

Teapot

Would you like a cup of tea?

Coffee Cup

School Bus

Backpack

Crayon

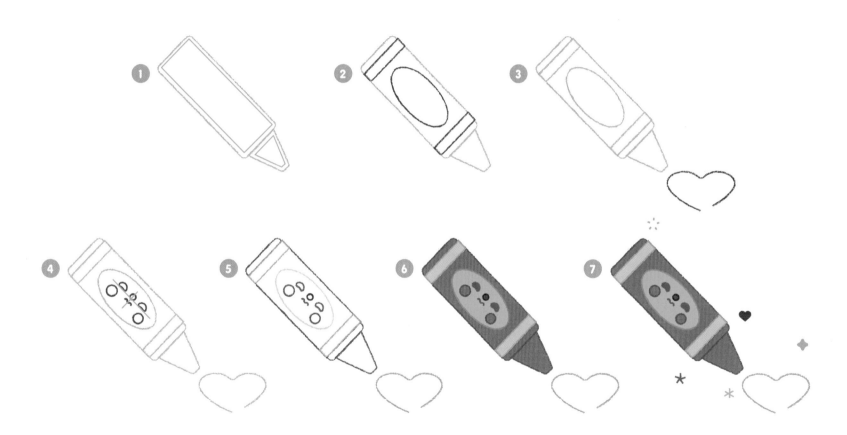

Pencil Pot

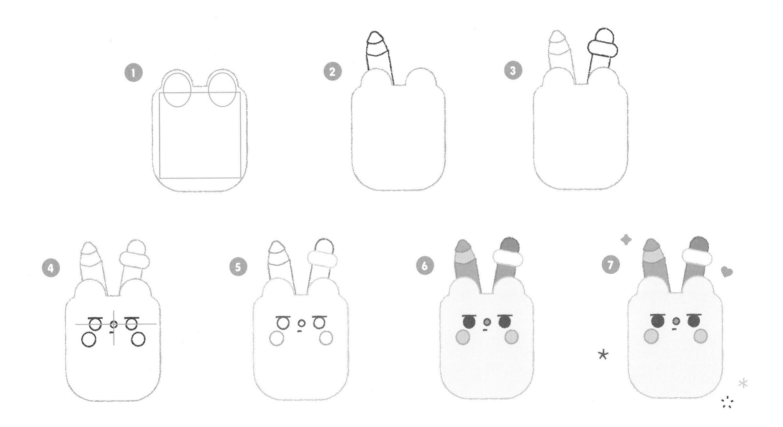

Closed Book

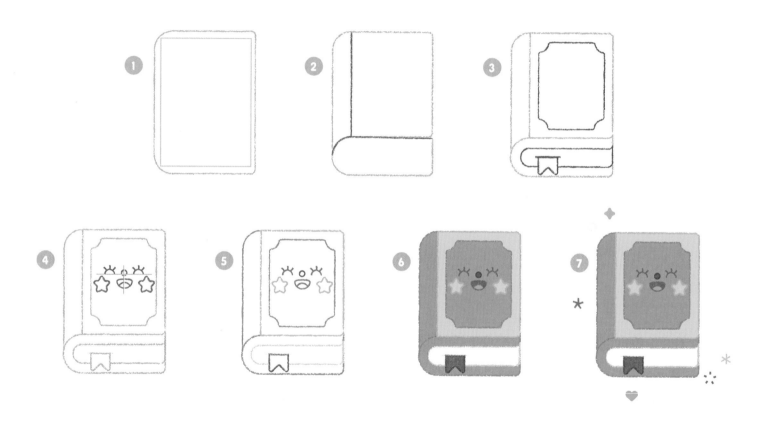

Open Book

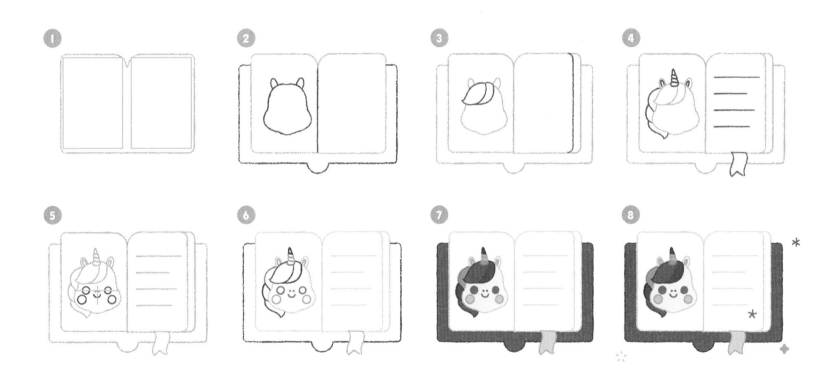

Sneaker

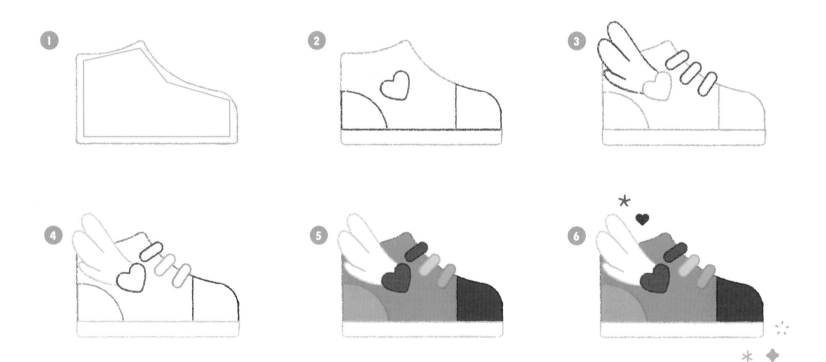

Sock

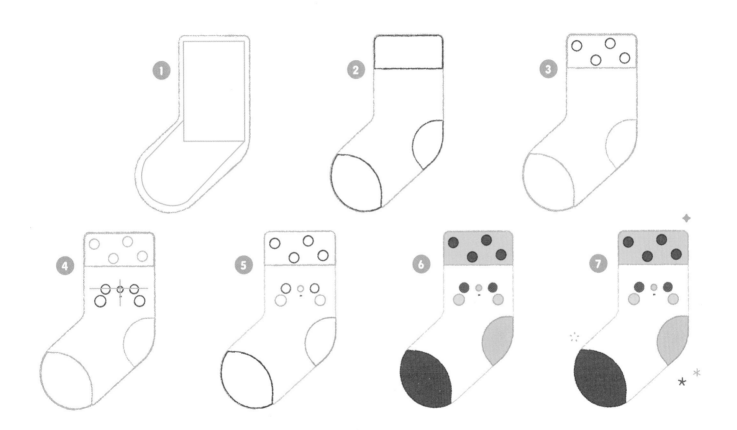

Baseball Cap

T-Shirt

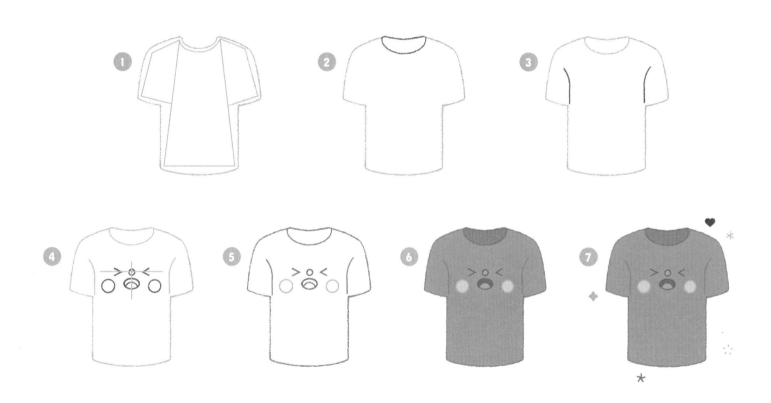

High Heel

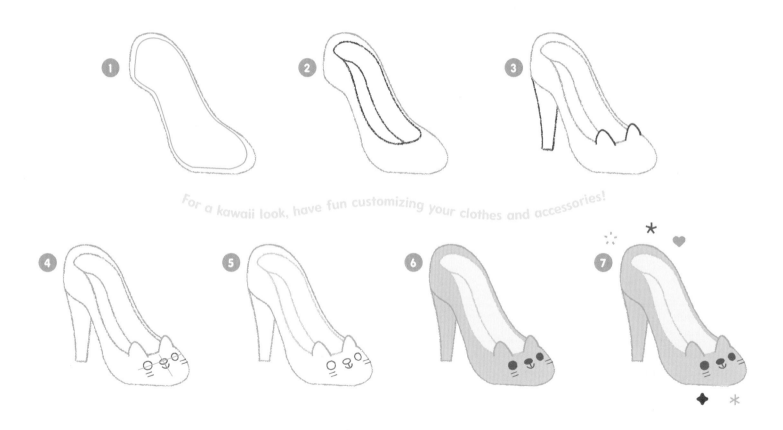

For a kawaii look, have fun customizing your clothes and accessories!

Lipstick

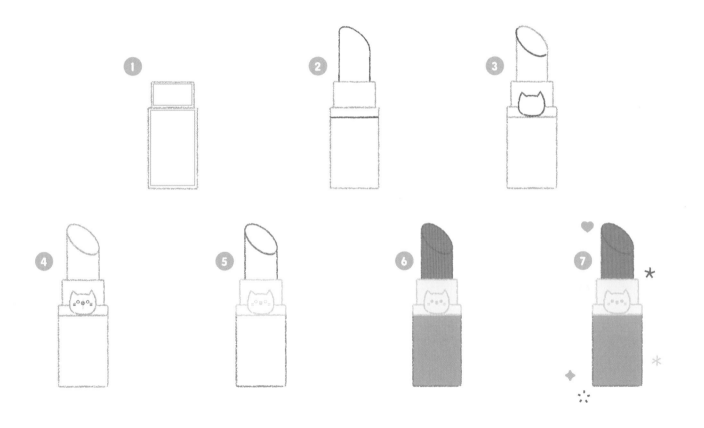

Perfume

Shopping Bag

Handbag

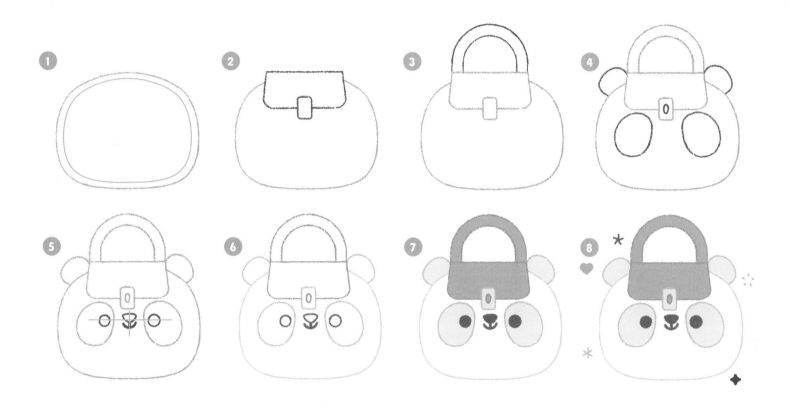

Love Letter

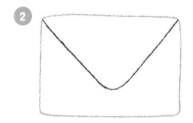

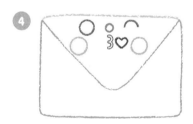

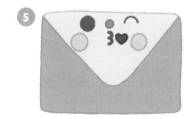

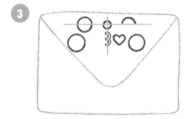

Headphones

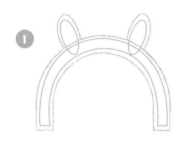

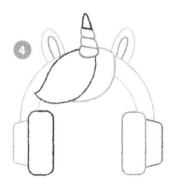

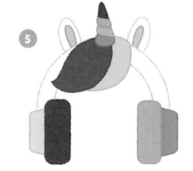

164

Rollerskate

Computer

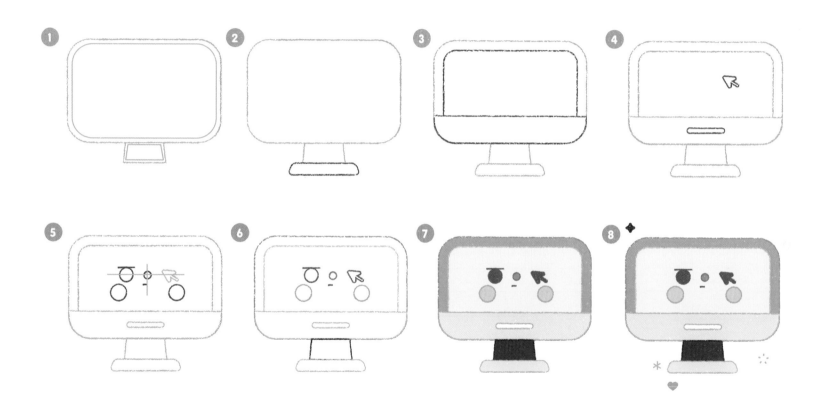

Cassette

Musical Notes

Electric Guitar

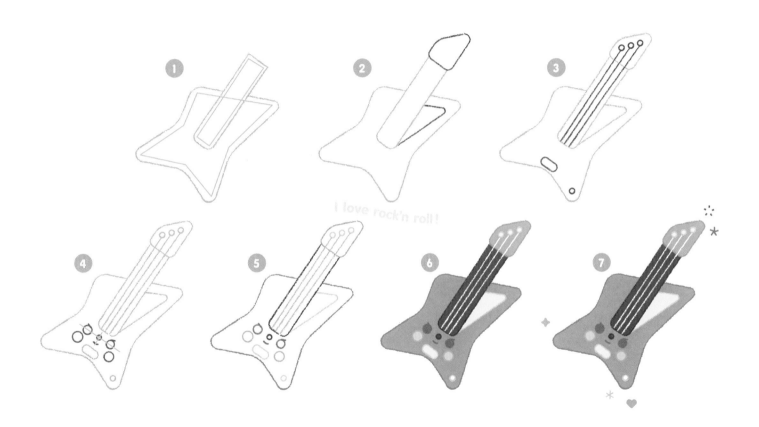

I love rock'n roll!

Drumkit

Drum

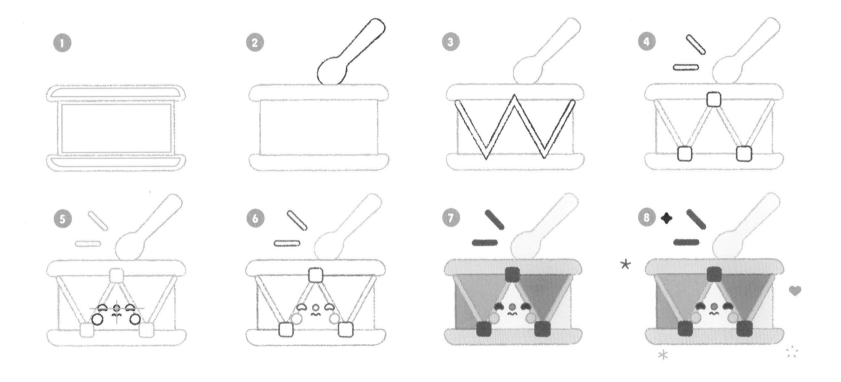

Keyboard

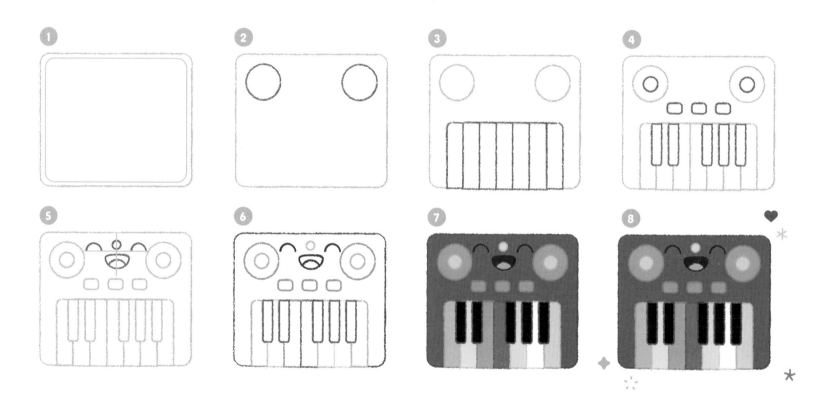

Trumpet

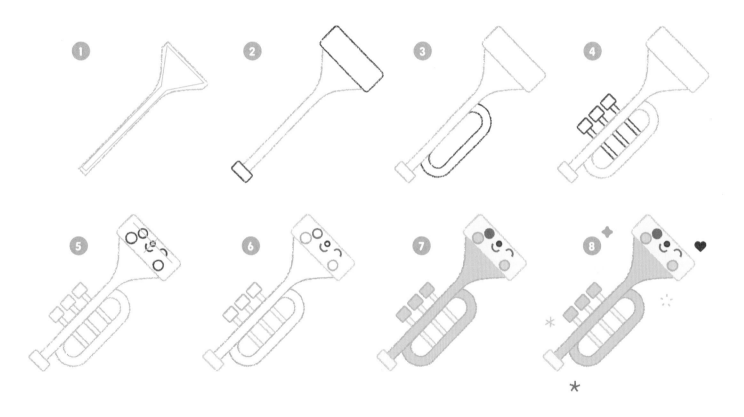

Umbrella

Cloud

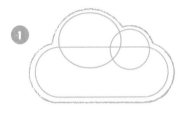

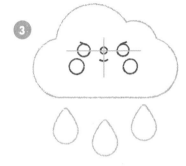

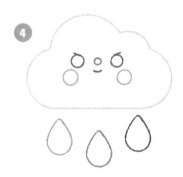

Rainbow Cloud

Storm Cloud

After the Rain

Sunshine

Shooting Star

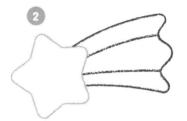

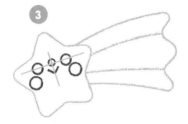

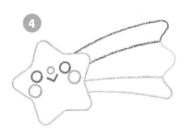

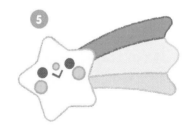

Waouh!

Bright Star

Starfish

1

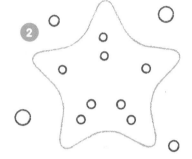

2

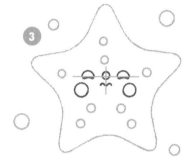

3

4

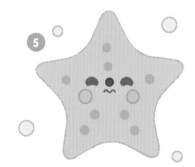

5

6

Coral

Unicorn Inflatable

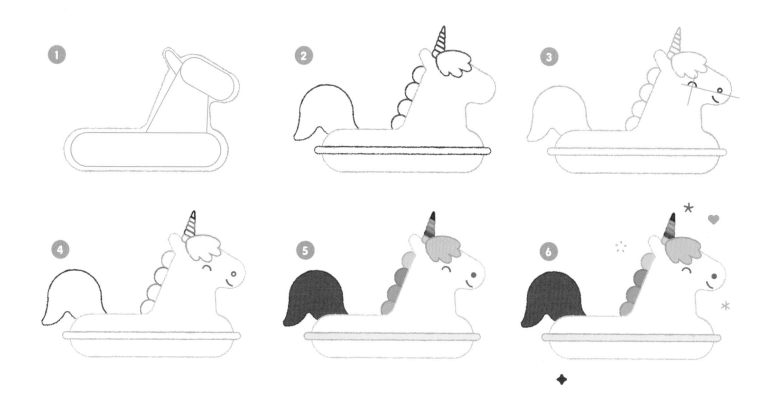

Flamingo Inflatable

Beach Ball

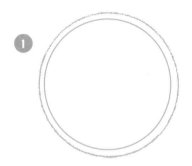

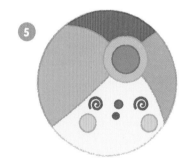

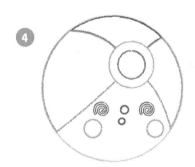

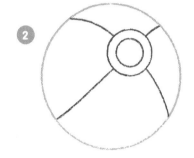

Bucket and Spade

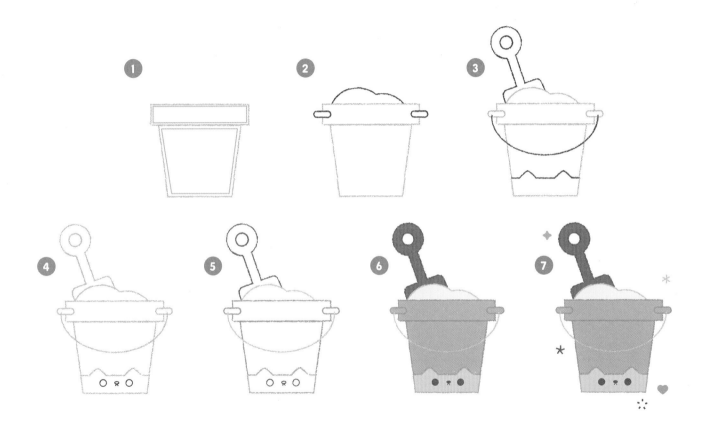

Wind Spinner

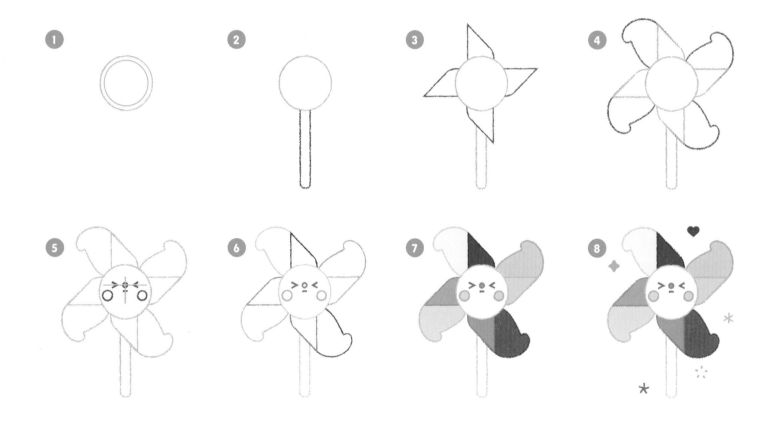

Hot Air Balloon

Simple Snowflake

Complex Snowflake

Christmas Tree

Gift Box

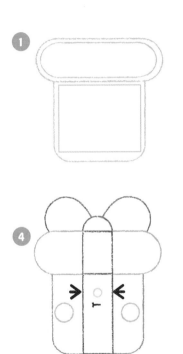

Merry Christmas!

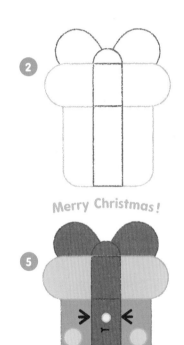

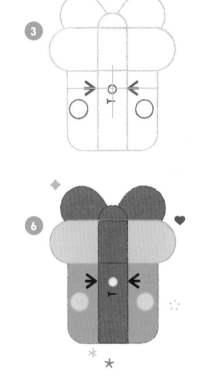

Striped Bauble

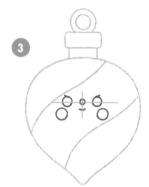

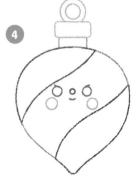

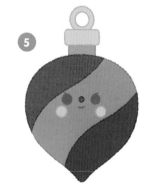

Scalloped Bauble

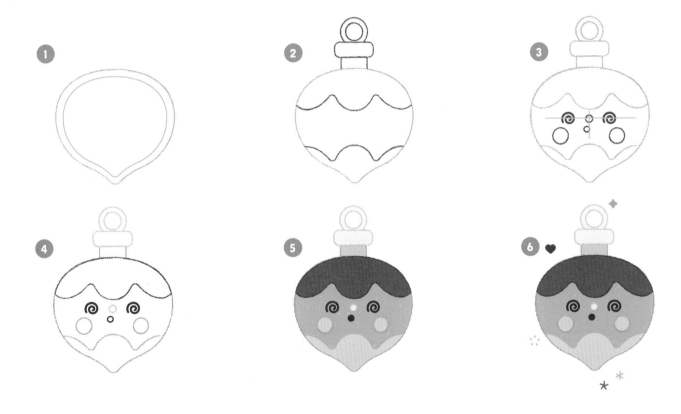

Candle

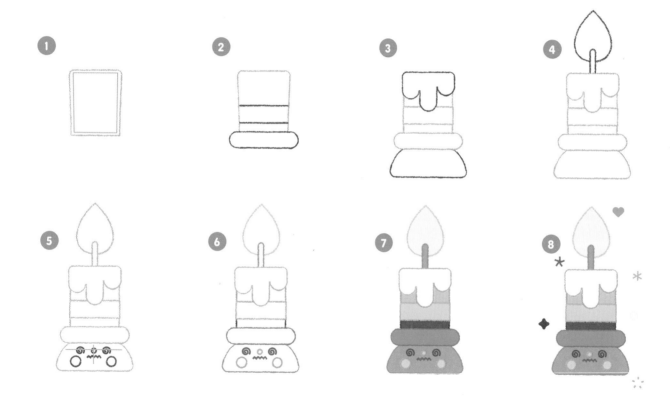

Light Bulb

Fairytale Castle

Magic Wand

King's Crown

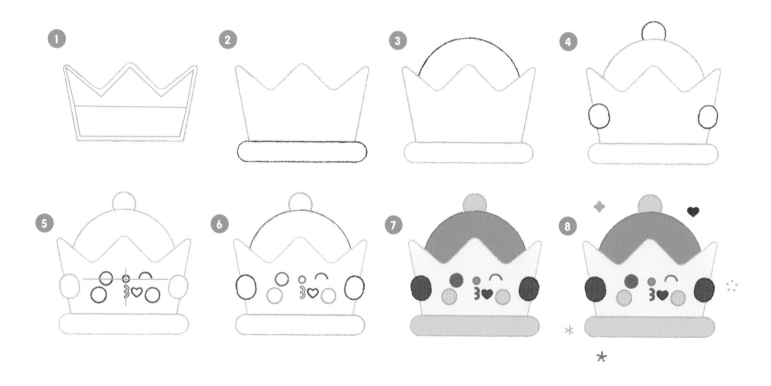

Queen's Crown

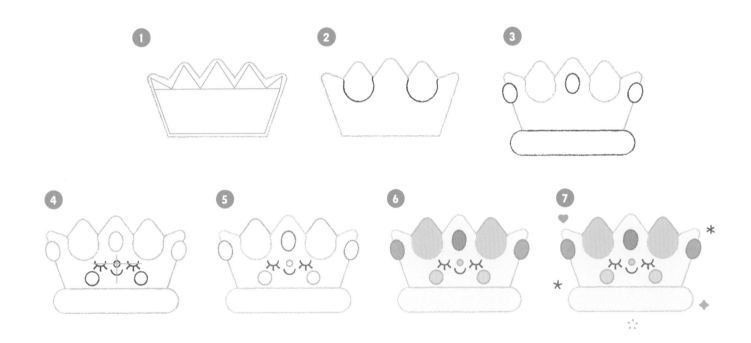

Love Potion

Magic Potion

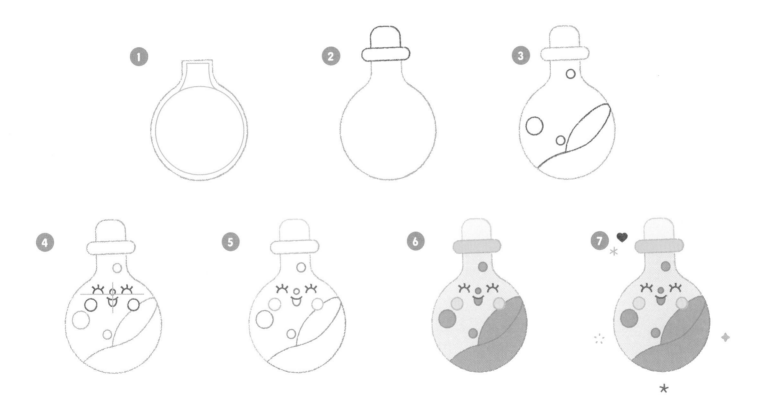

Chinese Lantern

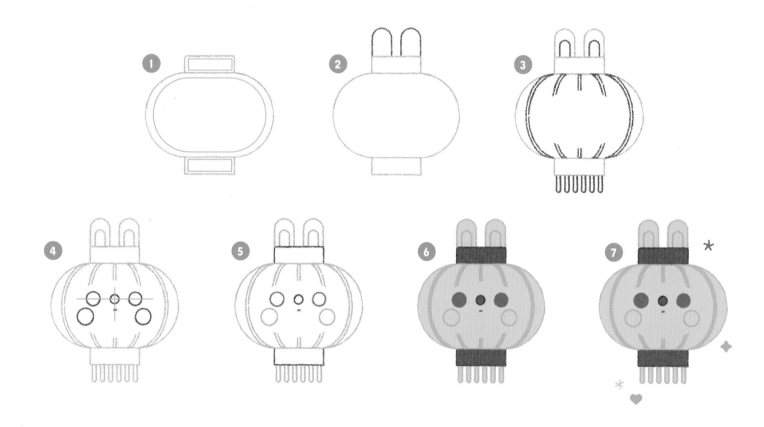

Beckoning Cat

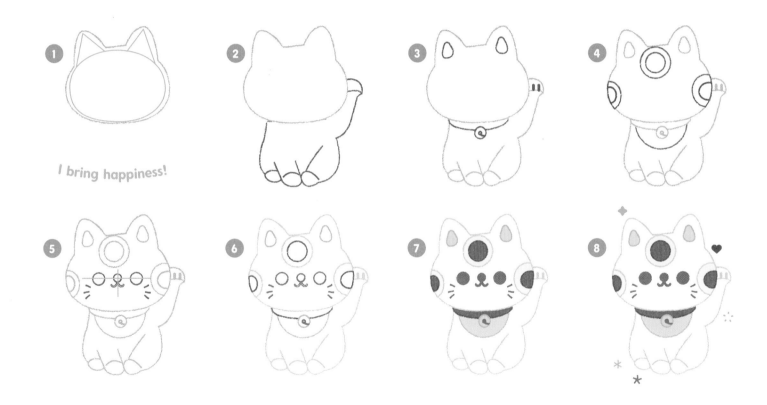

1

I bring happiness!

2

3

4

5

6

7

8

Kokeshi

Matryoshka

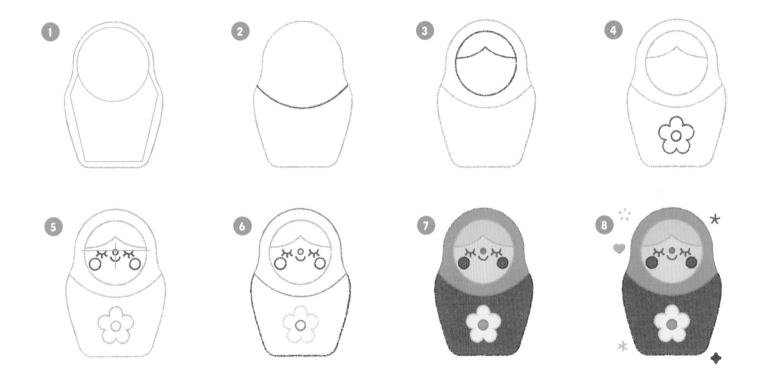

Dreamcatcher

Feather

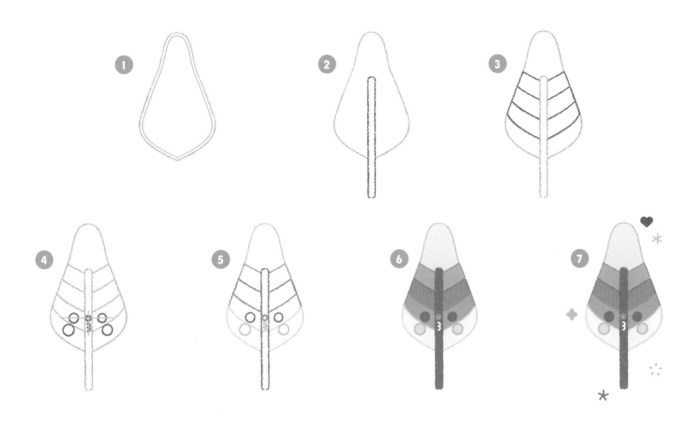

Tooth

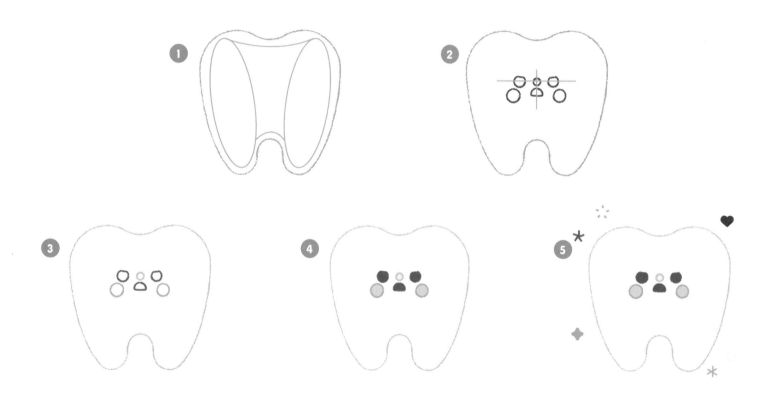

Toothbrush

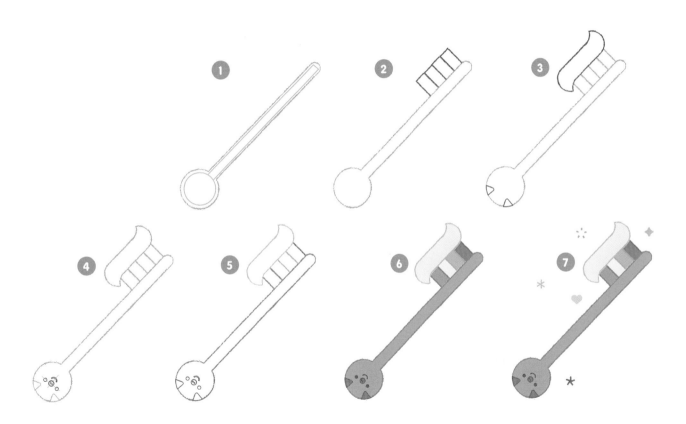

King Bear

Unicorns have lots of amazing friends!

Uni-Bear

Sitting Uni-Bear

Tanuki

Sitting Uni-Rabbit

Uni-Rabbit

217

Uni-Cat

Kitty King

Kitty Queen

Sitting Uni-Cat

Inu Hariko

Let yourself be protected by this companion who watches over children and future mothers!

Colourful Puppy

Poodle

Uni-Kitten

Uni-Puppy

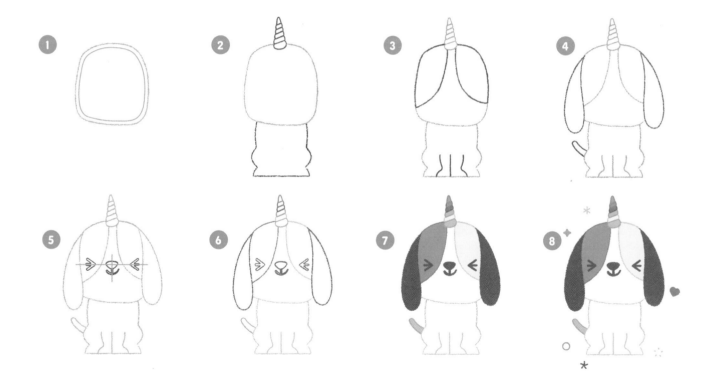

Kitty Princess

Pink Puppy

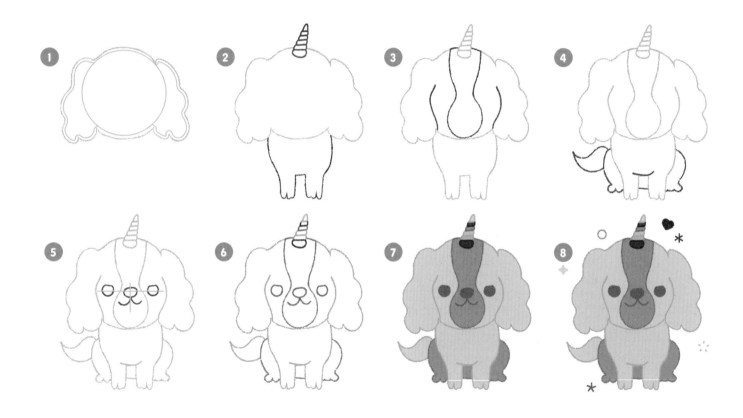

King Dog

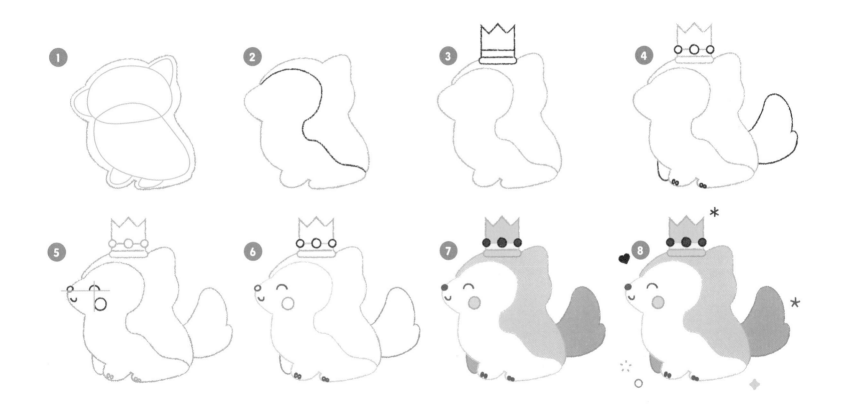

Sleeping Fox

Uni-Fox

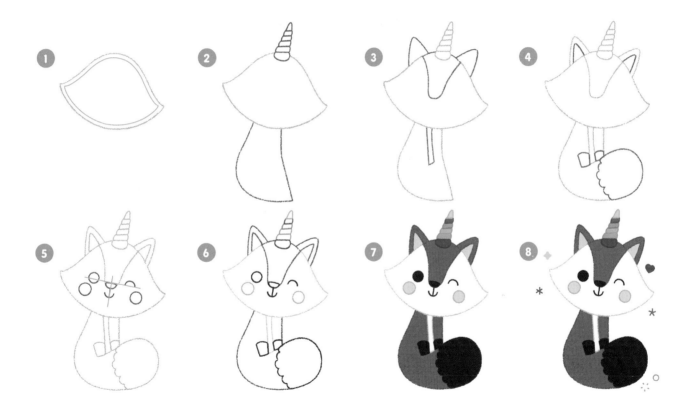

Reindeer

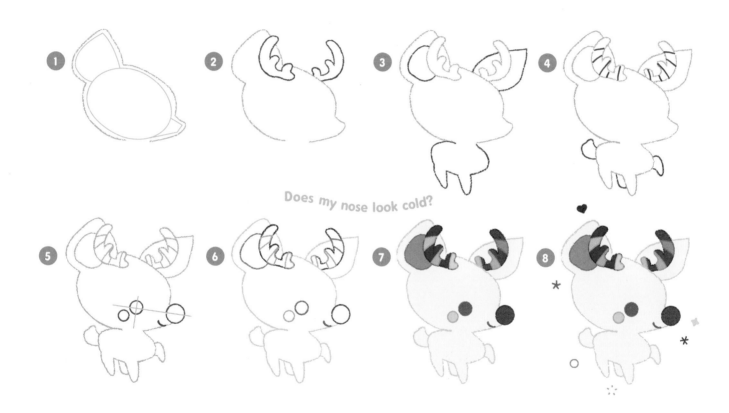

Does my nose look cold?

Fawn

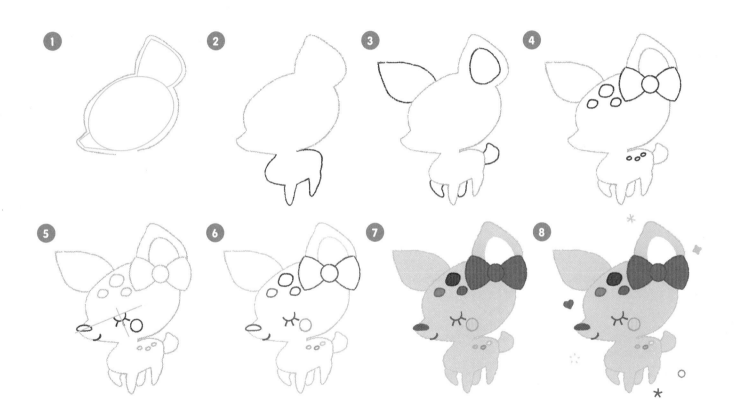

Squirrel

Raccoon

Wild Boar

Hedgehog

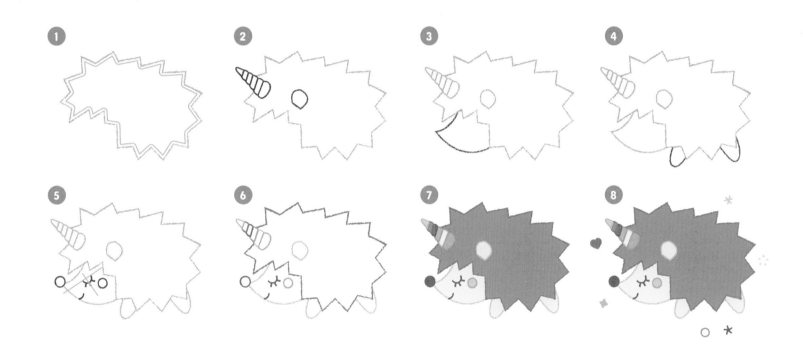

Uni-Pig

Party Pig

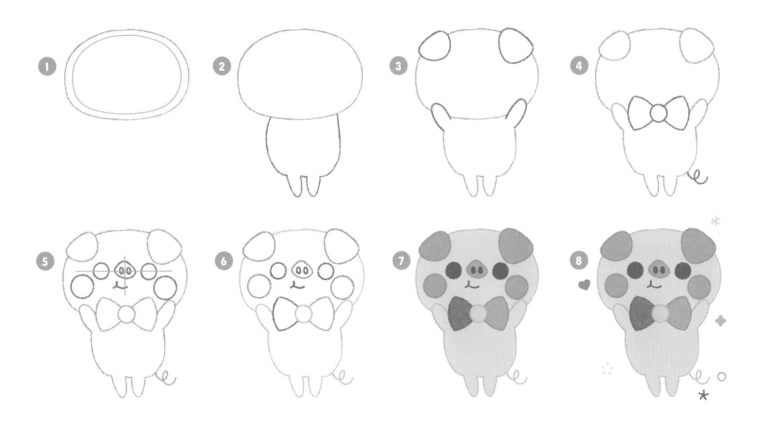

Sleepy Sheep

Cute Cow

Chicken

Uni-Chick

Sparrow

Uni-Bird

Kappa

Did you know this Japanese mythological animal is a big lover of cucumber?

246

Seagull

1

2

3

4

5

6

Uni-Kiwi

Uni-Llama

Uni-Sloth

Toucan

Pink Panda

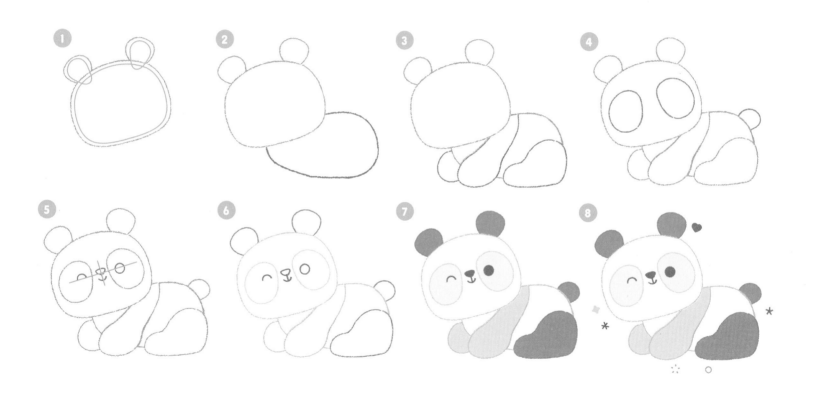

Dancing Panda

Sad Uni-Koala

Sleepy Uni-Koala

Uni-Monkey

Monkey King

Come on, don't pull faces!

Tiger

Lion

259

Rhino

Zebra

Elephant King

Uni-Phant

Uni-Bat

Giraffe

Uni-Seal

Uni-Sea Lion

Uni-Platypus

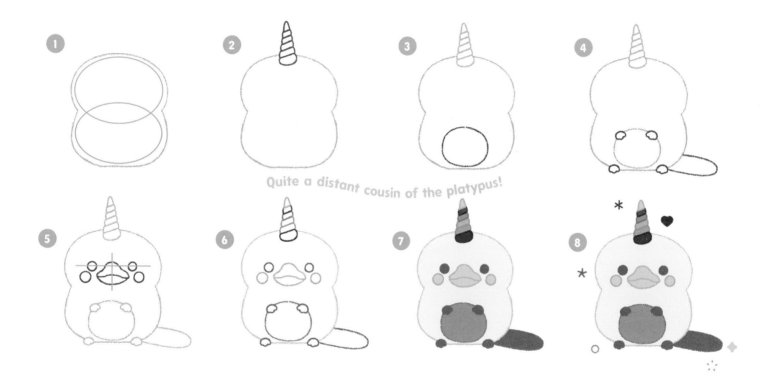

Quite a distant cousin of the platypus!

Uni-Otter

Uni-Penguin

Little Uni-Penguin

Swan Queen

Duck

Uni-Flamingo

Pink Dolphin

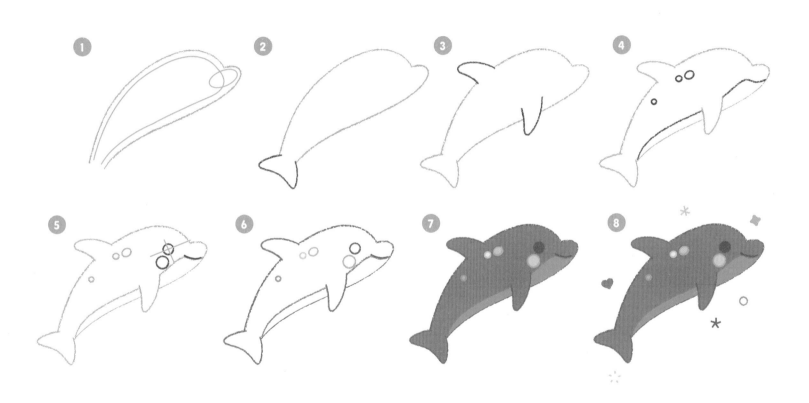

275

Uni-Narwhal

Uni-Shark

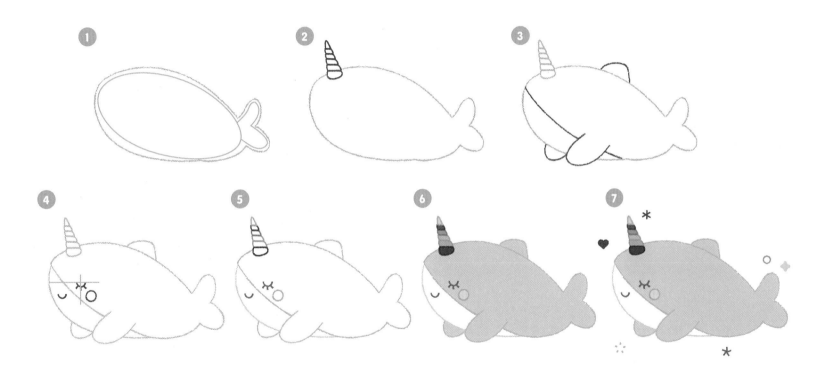

Uni-Jellyfish

Uni-Whale

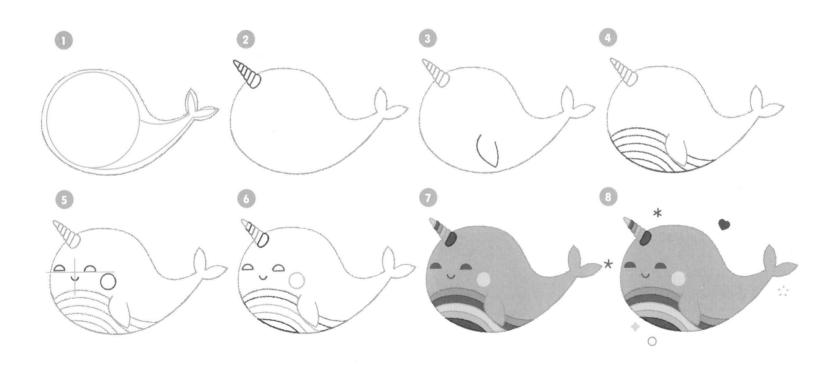

Axolotl

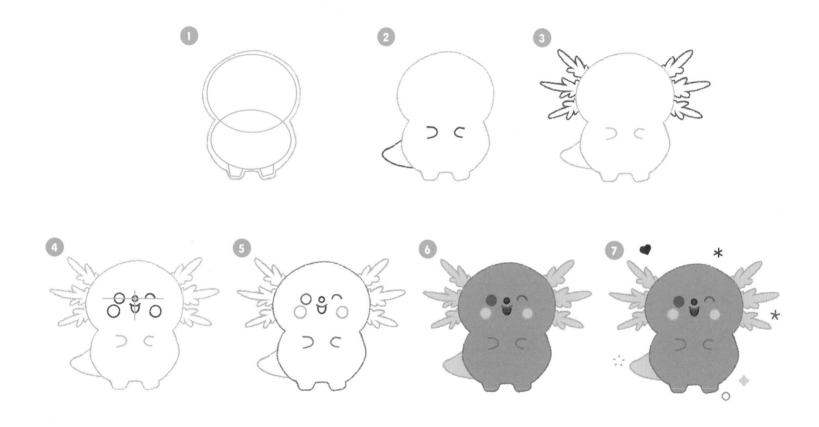

Moon Fish

Uni-Octopus

Royal Octopus

I'm the king of the ocean!

Rainbow Fish

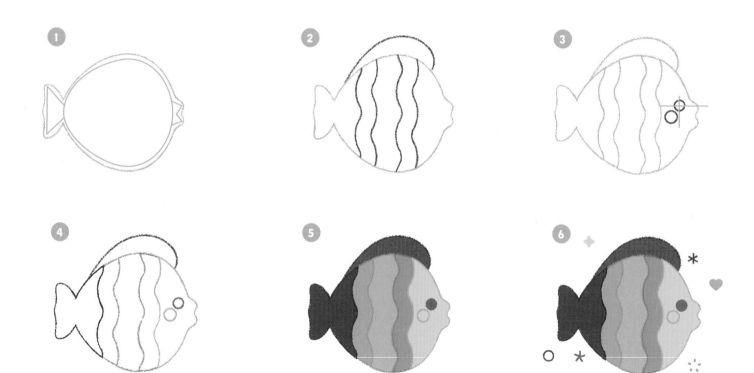

Rainbow Shrimp

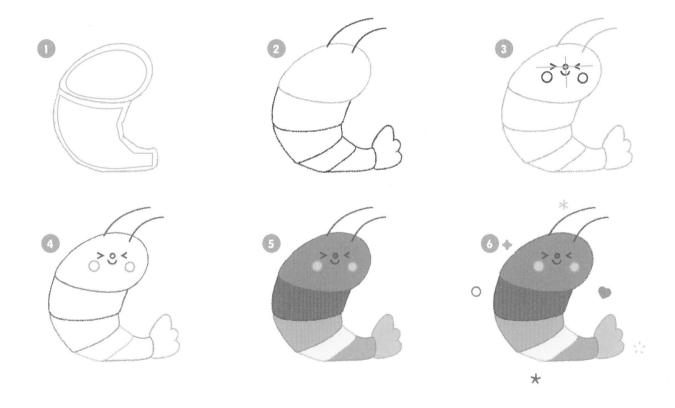

Uni-Fish

Uni-Seahorse

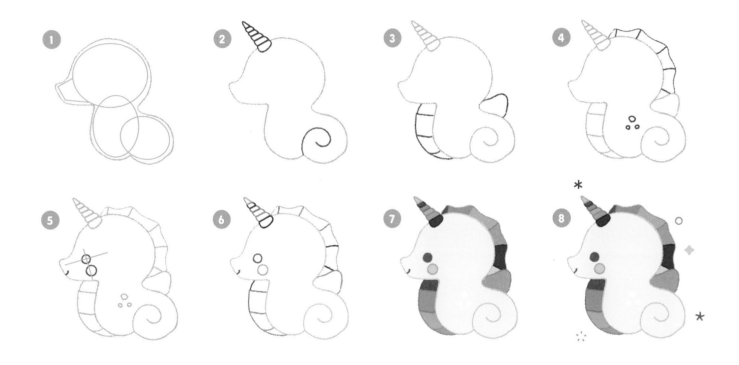

Uni-Turtle

Crocodile

Salamander

Frog Prince

Snake King

Uni-Dinosaur

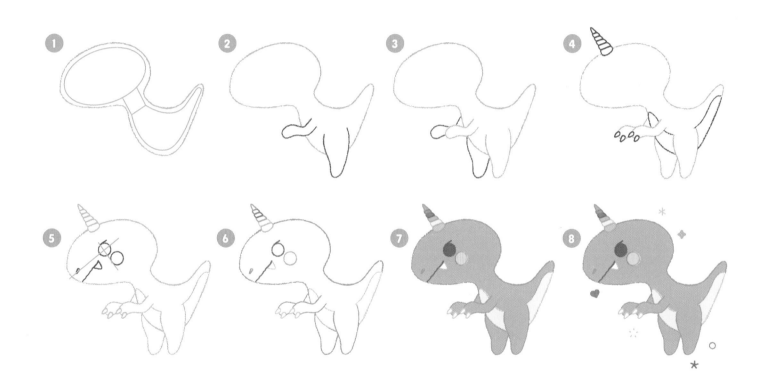

Crab

Snail

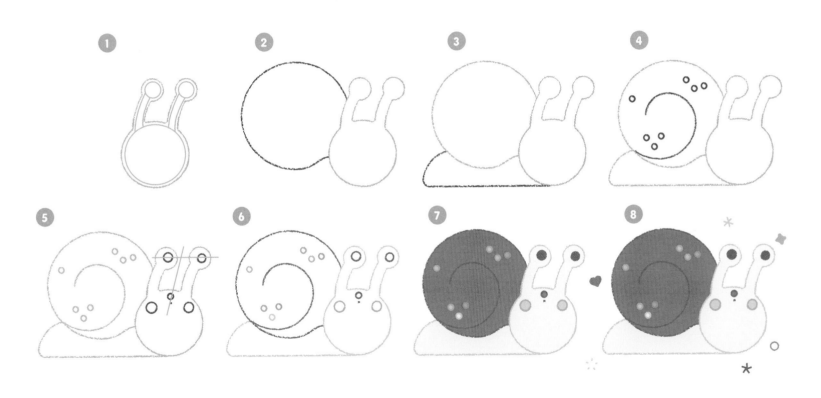

Uni-Worm

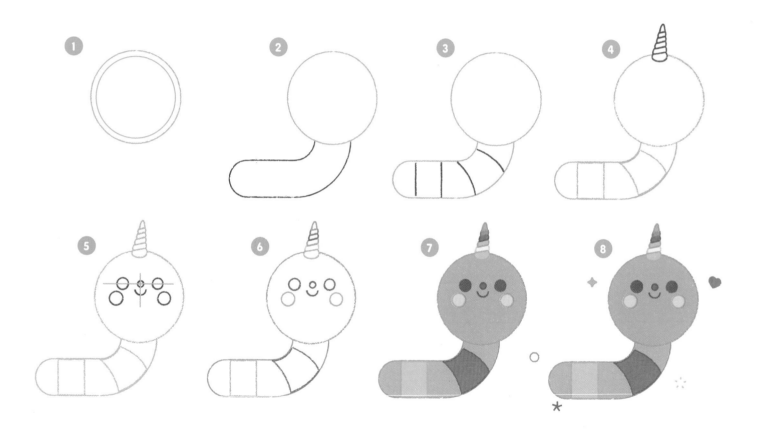

Ladybird

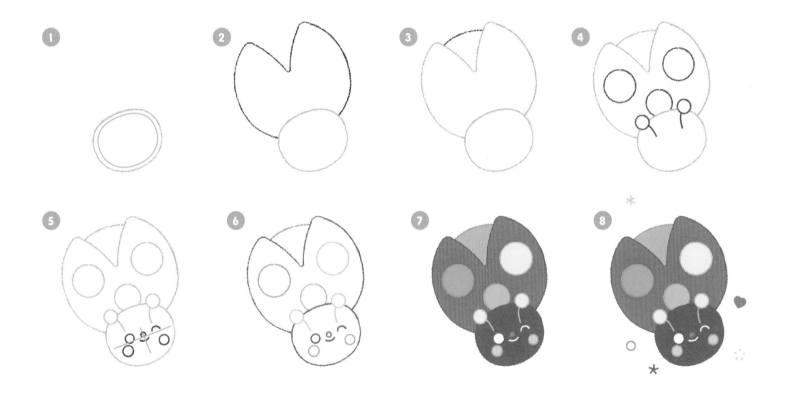

Butterfly

Bee

A is for Alligator

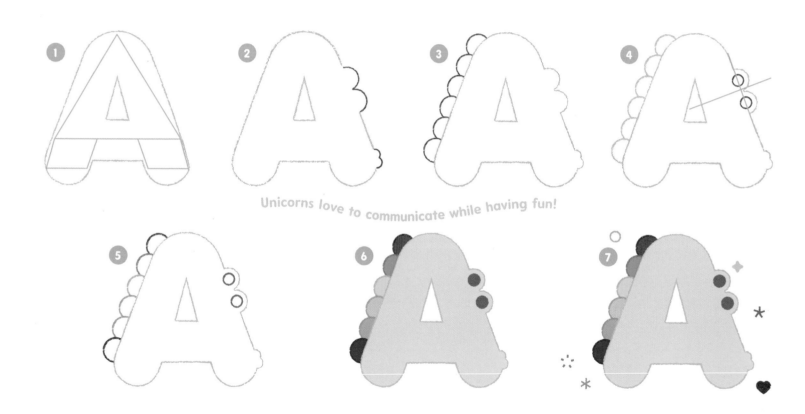

Unicorns love to communicate while having fun!

300

B is for Baboon

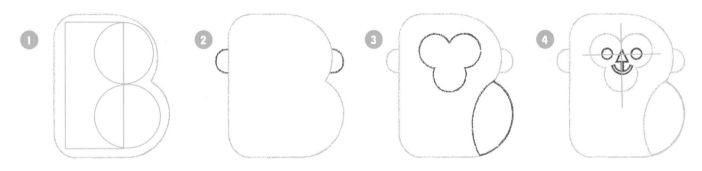

They transform all the letters of the alphabet!

C is for Cat

D is for Deer

E is for Elephant

F is for Flamingo

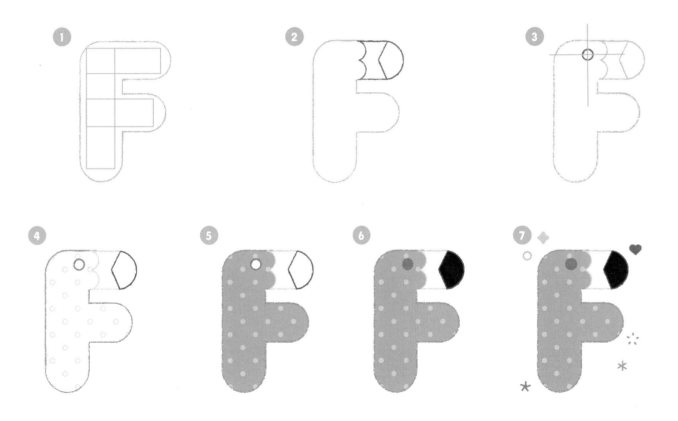

G is for Giraffe

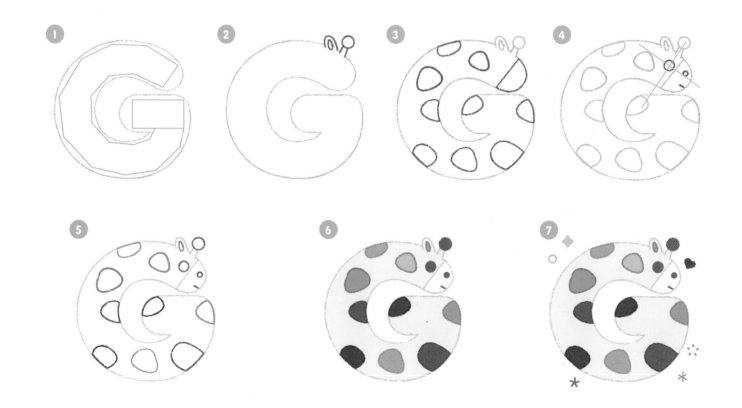

H is for Hippo

I is for Iguana

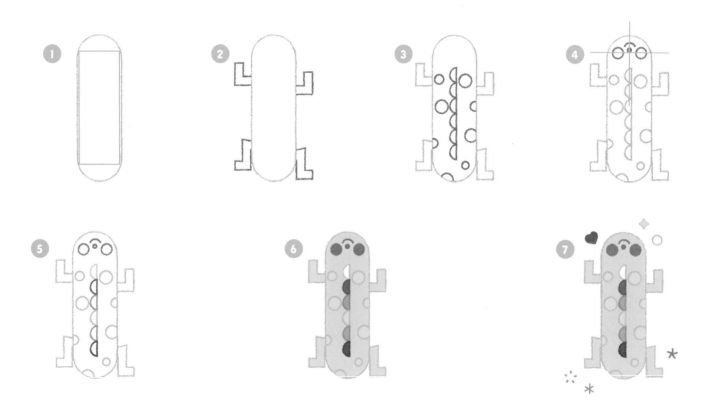

J is for Jellyfish

K is for Koala

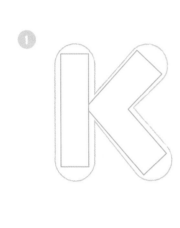

L is for Lion

M is for Mouse

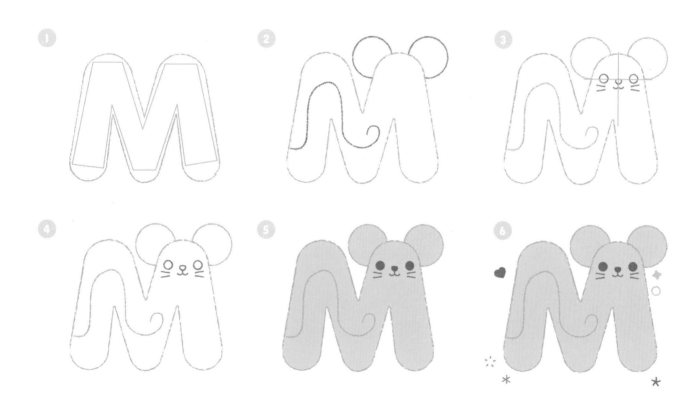

N is for Narwhal

O is for Owl

P is for Panda

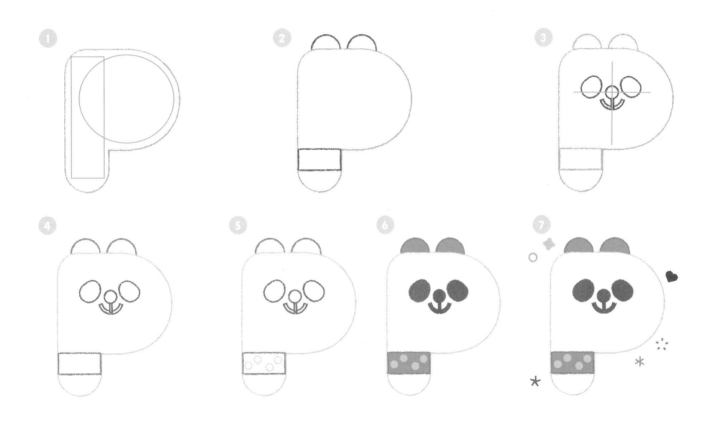

Q is for Quokka

R is for Rhino

S is for Snake

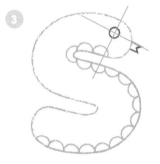

318

T is for Tiger

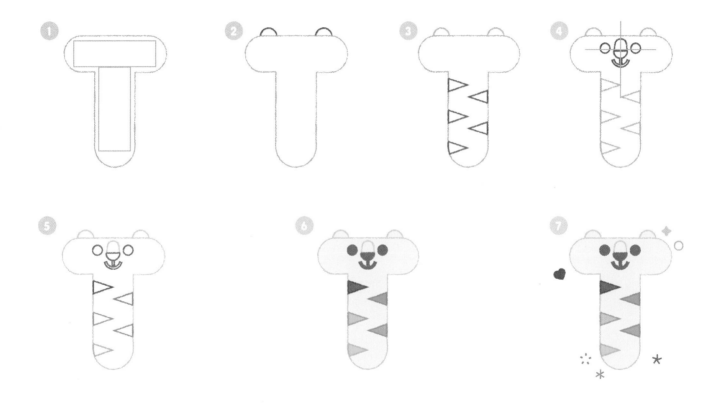

U is for Umbrella Bird

V is for Vulture

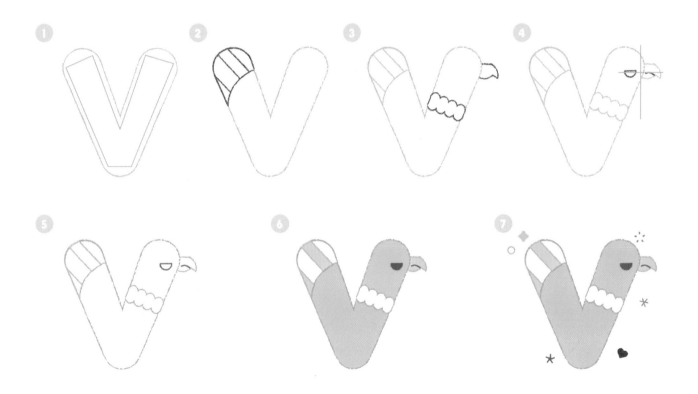

W is for Wombat

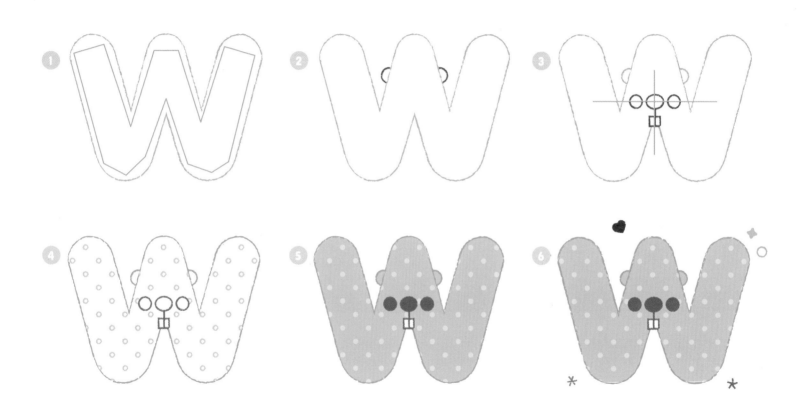

X is for X-ray Fish

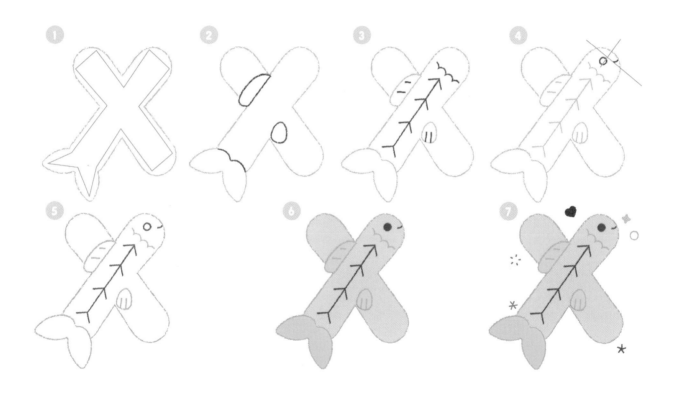

Y is for Yak

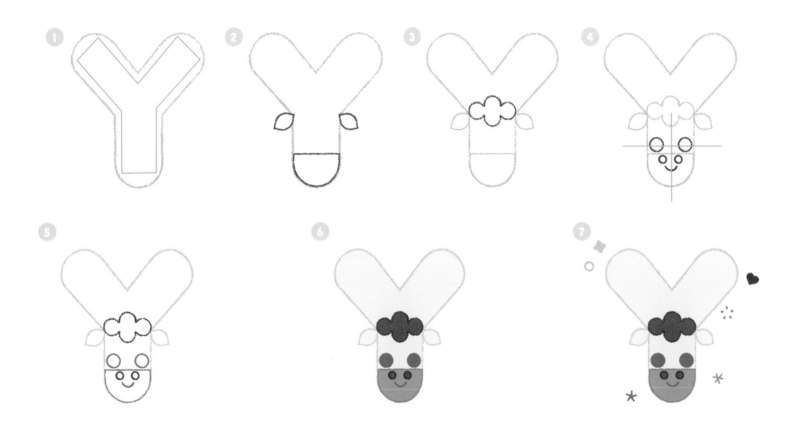

Z is for Zebra

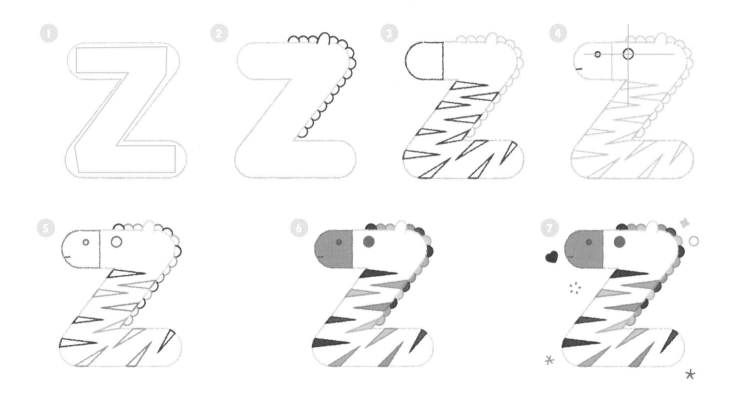

Exclamation Mark

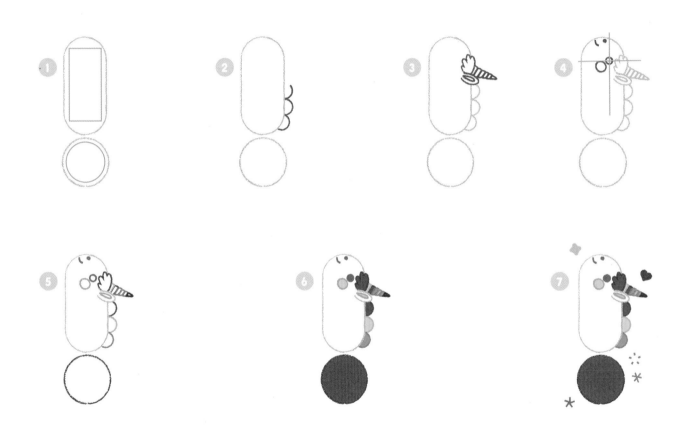

Question Mark

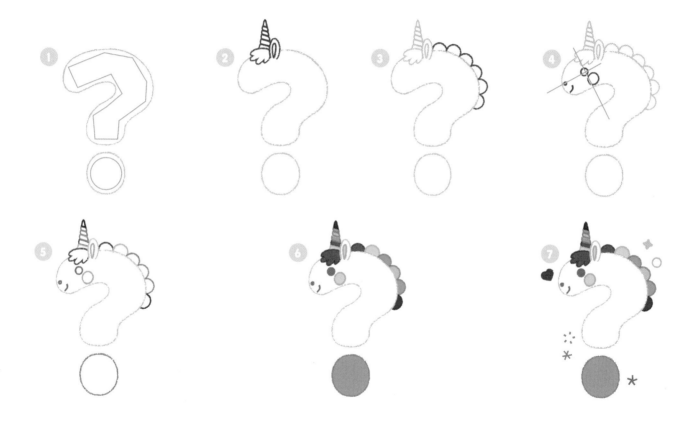

At Symbol

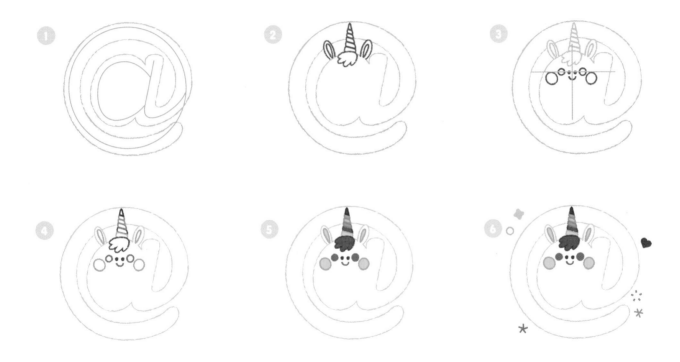

328

Hashtag

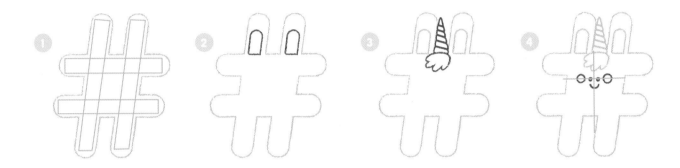

Zero

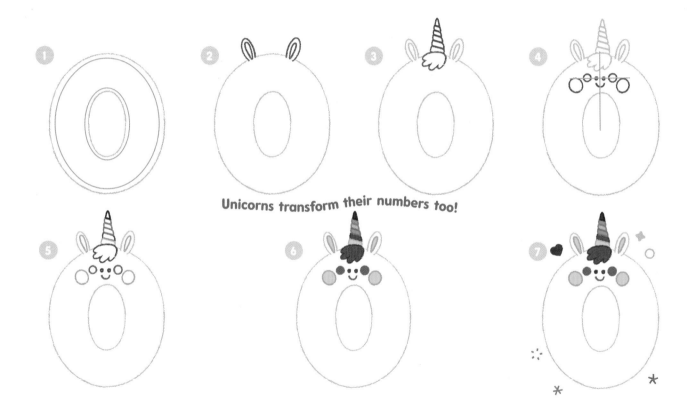

Unicorns transform their numbers too!

One

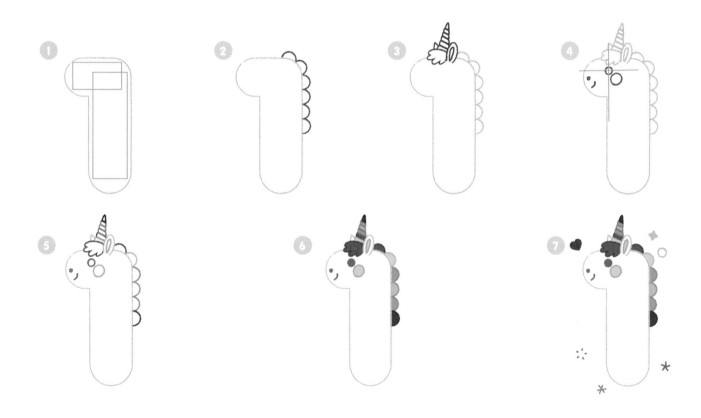

Two

Three

Four

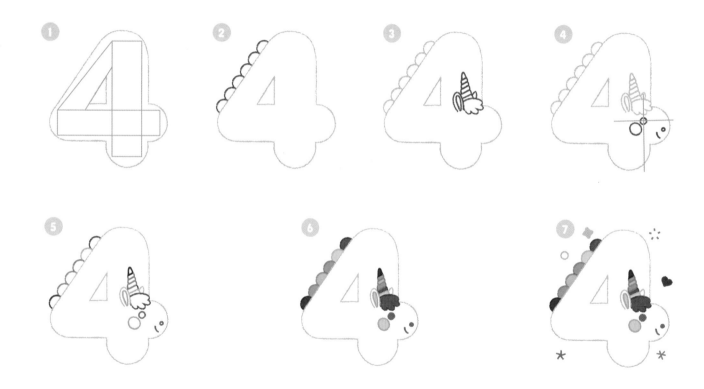

Five

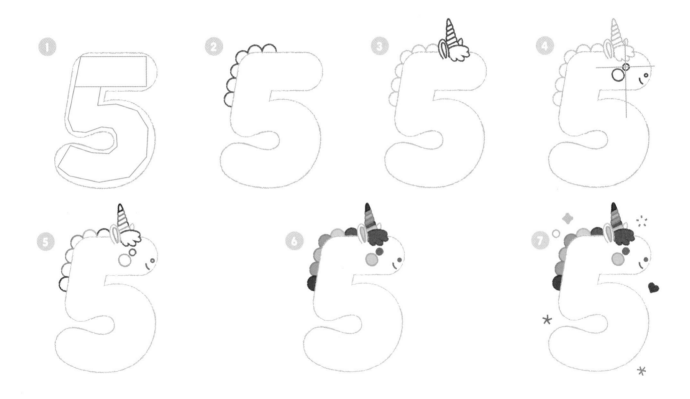

Six

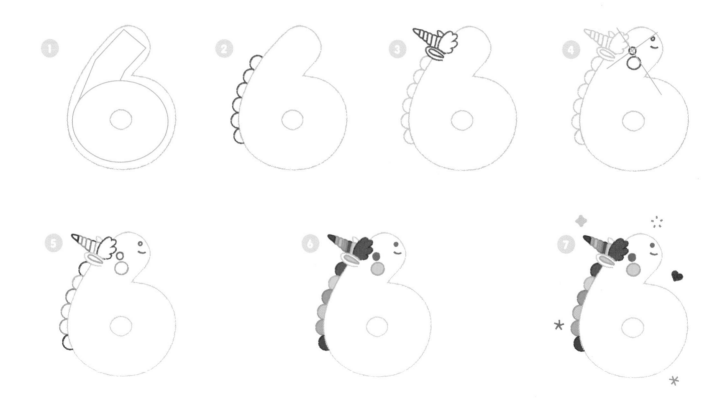

Seven

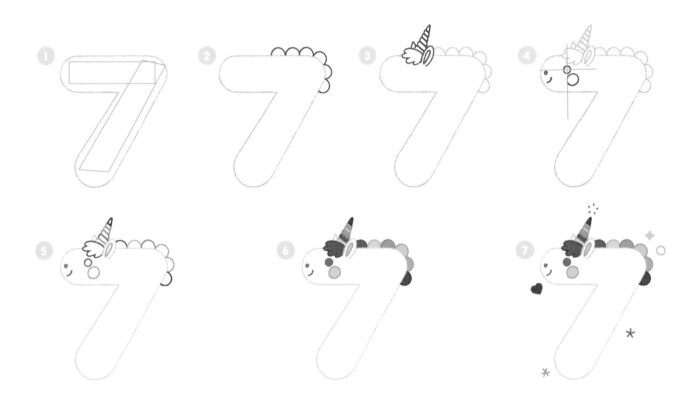

Eight

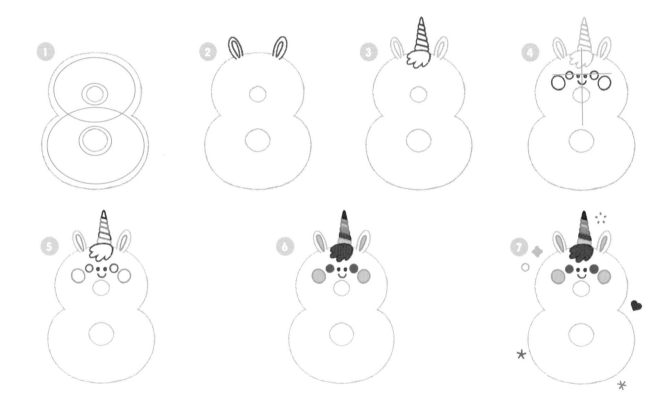

338

Nine

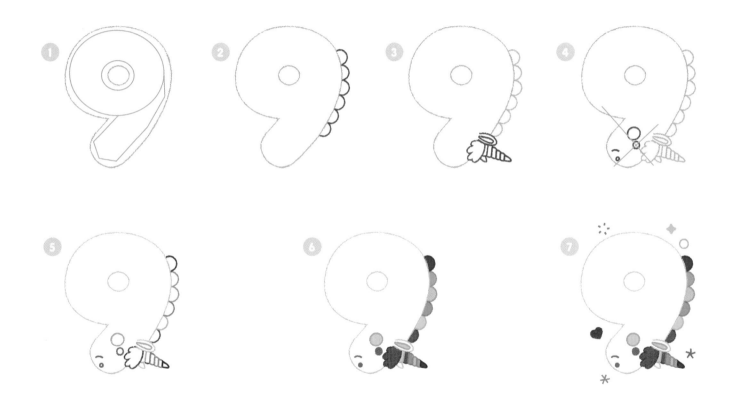

339

Year of the Dog

Find your animal mascot according to Chinese astrology!

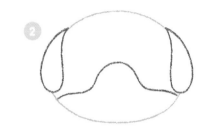

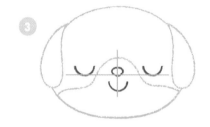

You are a dog if you were born in 1970, 1982, 1994 or 2006.

A loyal and endearing friend, the dog knows how to avoid many traps!

Year of the Pig

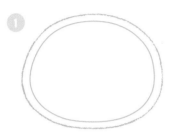

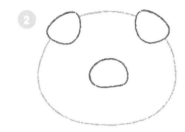

You are pig if you were born in 1971, 1983, 1995 or 2007.

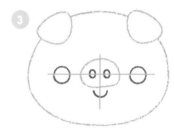

Calm and honest, the pig is a precious friend!

Year of the Rat

You are a rat if you were born in 1972, 1984, 1996 or 2008.

The rat is secretive and brings good luck to those around it!

Year of the Cow

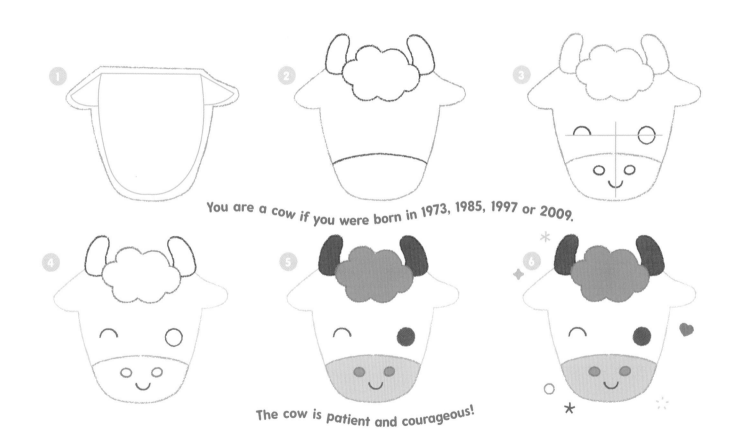

You are a cow if you were born in 1973, 1985, 1997 or 2009.

The cow is patient and courageous!

343

Year of the Tiger

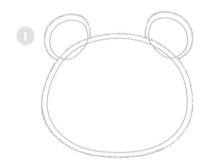

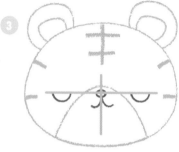

You are a tiger if you were born in 1974, 1986, 1998 or 2010.

The tiger is a real go-getter!

Year of the Rabbit

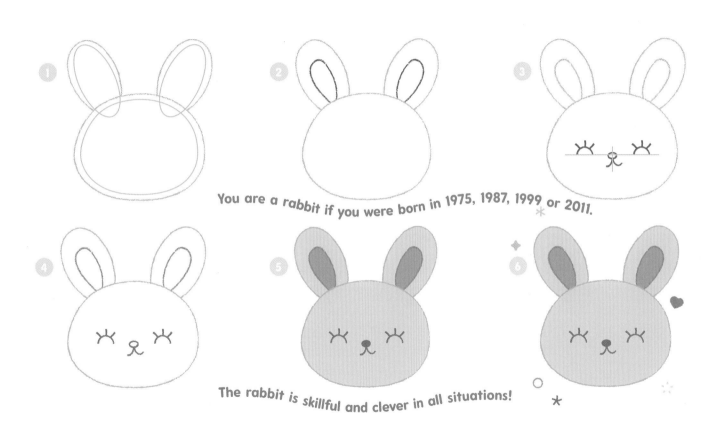

You are a rabbit if you were born in 1975, 1987, 1999 or 2011.

The rabbit is skillful and clever in all situations!

Year of the Dragon

You are a dragon if you were born in 1976, 1988, 2000 or 2012.

Irresistible, the dragon is a star!

346

Year of the Snake

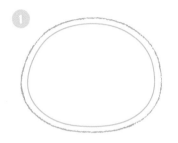

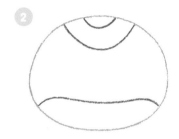

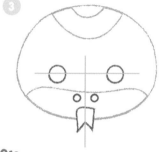

You are a snake if you were born in 1977, 1989, 2001 or 2013.

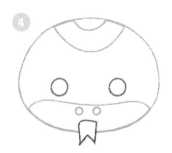

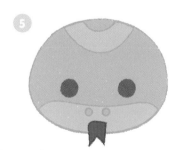

The snake is a symbol of wisdom!

Year of the Horse

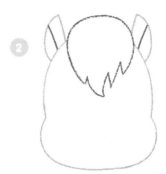

You are a horse if you were born in 1978, 1990, 2002 or 2014.

The horse likes to explore new horizons!

348

Year of the Goat

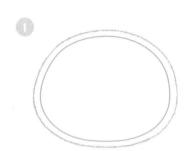

You are a goat if you were born in 1979, 1991, 2003 or 2015.

Very creative, the goat is a real artist!

Year of the Monkey

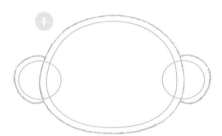

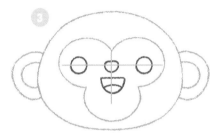

You are a monkey if you were born in 1980, 1992, 2004 or 2016.

Spreading the joy of life, the monkey is never short of ideas!

350

Year of the Rooster

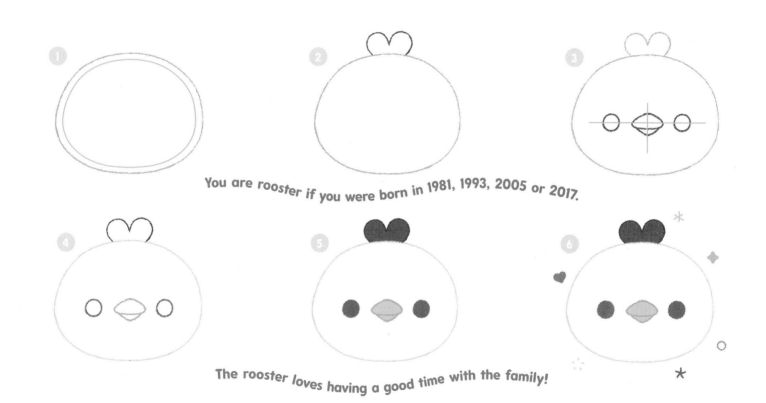

You are rooster if you were born in 1981, 1993, 2005 or 2017.

The rooster loves having a good time with the family!

Unicorn Emoticons

Unicorns even invented their own emoticons to express their emotions!

Hello!

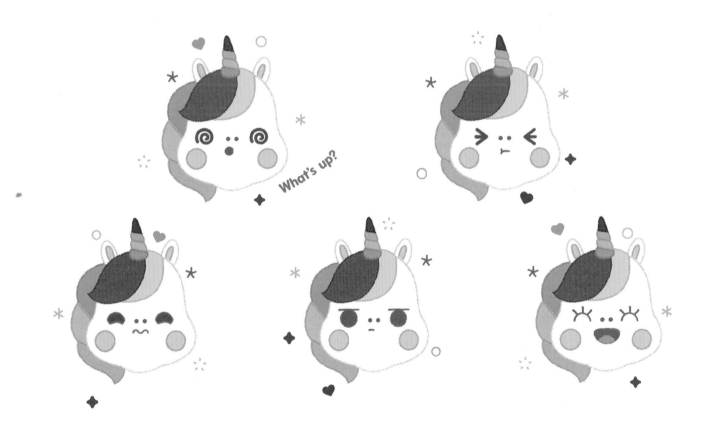

What's up?

I love it!

Ohhh!

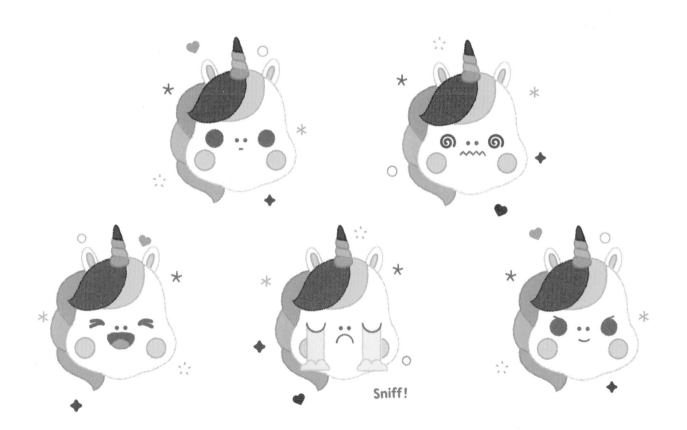

Sniff!

Say it...

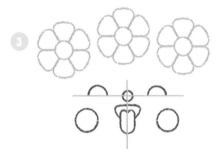

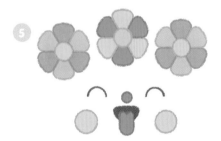

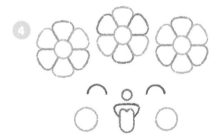

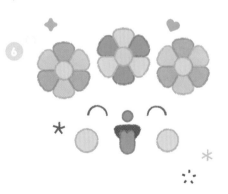

...with Flowers!

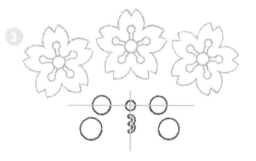

359

Little Heart...

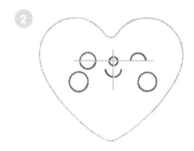

...with a Bow!

Heart Banner

Flower Rosette

Double Bow

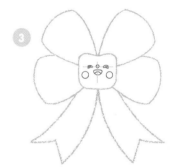

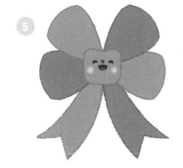

Striped Bow

Bunting

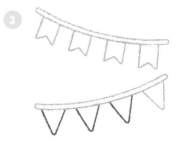

366

Banner

Goodbye!

Hope you liked this book. Mwah!